Getting a
YES
to Your
PRAYERS

*366 Petitions in Full Agreement
with God's Will*

Jan Dargatz Ph.D.

Pengold Garrett

© 2012 Jan Dargatz

Scripture references in this book are from:

The King James Version of the Bible (KJV).

The New King James Version of the Bible (NKJV), Thomas Nelson Publishers, Nashville, TN, 1982.

The New American Standard Bible (NAS), The Lockman Foundation, La Habra, California, 1995.

Prayer quotations are from *The New Dictionary of Thoughts* (Standard Book Company, 1963) and *God's Little Instruction Book on Prayer.* (Honor Books, 1996)

All rights reserved. No part of this book may be reproduced in any form or by any electronic or mechanical means, including information storage and retrieval systems, without permission in writing from the publisher, except by a reviewer who may quote brief passages in a review.

Publisher: Pengold Garrett & Associates, P.O. Box 702870, Tulsa, OK 74170.

Cover art and interior design: Starr Clay

ISBN: 978-1-937566-16-6

FOR

Joe
with thanksgiving for our many conversations about
prayer and intercession, and for inspiring us
to pray for one another at our church

and

Nancy and Charlene—
these are the prayers I first
wrote as prayers for you

and

those who attend my adult Sunday
School class and to my fellow
Daughters of the Holy Cross—
these are among the general
prayers I pray for you
with regularity!

Getting a
YES
to Your
PRAYERS

TABLE OF CONTENTS

1   HOW DO WE GET TO YES IN OUR PRAYERS? 1

2   PRAYERS WITH SCRIPTURES AND INSIGHTS 5

ABOUT THE AUTHOR 271

1 HOW DO WE GET TO YES IN OUR PRAYERS?

The answer is rooted in the way Jesus taught His followers to pray:

"Your kingdom come.

Your will be done,

On earth as it is in heaven."

(Mathew 6:10 NAS)

The will of Heaven is that the principles of God's kingdom—which are the principles that are in full operation in Heaven—be established on this earth. Prayer is petition. It is ASKING God for those things we need to fulfill our purpose on this earth. It is also ASKING God for all those things He desires to give us! Our primary role in prayer is to ASK God for His kingdom and His will to be established FULLY in the here and now of our lives.

The prayers that produce a SURE "yes" answer from God are those that are in line with God's will. And to that end, they must be prayers that are totally in line with God's Word. God's will and God's Word are in complete alignment. Never assume otherwise. We err greatly any time we ask God to provide or bless anything that He prohibits in His Word.

Throughout Scripture, we find verses that tell us very plainly what God desires for us to DO—how to believe, think, speak, and act. Those are the verses that are directly applicable to all petitions for ourselves and intercession for others! We also find verses that are general promises to ALL who love and seek to obey the Lord. These promises are also a sure foundation for prayer. What God has said, and what God has promised, are expressions of what God desires to do . . . and what God desires to do, God *will* do.

Why ask? If God can perform His will anytime and anywhere, and if He knows what is best for us, why do we have to ask? Because the Bible tells us to ask! Asking is a vital aspect of God's gift of free will to all human beings. We have a choice to turn to Him, or turn away. We have a choice to depend on God, or seek to live life according to our own will. Prayer—petitioning, asking—is the prime expression of our saying to God, "I seek this from YOU. I am asking YOU to be the Source of all that is good, beneficial, and blessed in my life."

James 4:2 tells us simply, "You do not have because you do not ask." (NAS) Asking focuses our faith, and it also reveals to us more about our true intentions and desires. God already knows what we need. He wants US to know that He is the Source of our provision.

Many times people receive a blessing from God or an answer to prayer and then say, "I can't believe it! Guess what just happened?" Why are they surprised? After all, they *asked* for what they received. God wants us to connect the dots! He wants us to see that our requests and His answers are connected. What we ask of God becomes some form of answer FROM God. His answer may be "no." It may be "later." It may be "do this first." It may be, "I have something better." And sometimes it is a resounding YES!

When we ask, however, God always ANSWERS.

What happens when we ask in agreement with God's Word—not only believing His commandment but doing them? The promise of God's Word is that we RECEIVE what we request! 1 John 3:22 tells us, "Whatever we ask we receive from Him, because we keep His *commandments* and do the things that are pleasing in His sight." (NAS; italics added for emphasis)

Why then don't we get everything we request? James gives us insight into this as well: "You ask and do not receive, because you ask with wrong motives, so that you may spend it on your pleasures." (James 4:3 NAS) If your prayers aren't being answered with a resounding YES, ask God to reveal to you your motives. Also be aware that not all prayers are answered on our timetable or according to our desired methods. There may be prerequisite changes in your obedience that are keeping a YES answer from arriving. The timing may not be right. You might also be missing God's YES because you are looking for it to come through the wrong method or from the wrong person.

About this Book

This book was written to help a person BEGIN to see how God's Word and prayer petitions go together. You'll find 366 entries—one for each day of the year, including leap year. For each entry, you'll find a portion of Scripture, a statement of inspiration, instruction, or insight into the Scripture passage, and then, a prayer based upon the Word of God. The "heading" for each day is the overall theme or the "prayer request" (petition).

These prayers are for all people of all cultures at all times, both young and old, male and female, without any regard to race, religious denomination, or nationality. They are, however, decidedly CHRISTIAN prayers. They are prayers you can fully pray in the name of Jesus—because they are prayers in keeping with the character, ministry, and purposes of Jesus.

At times, the prayers are couched in "he and him" terms, at times in "she and her" terms. All of the prayers are equally applied to both men and women!

You may find that some of these entries are useful for sharing in group settings. From time to time, you may be asked to open or close a meeting in prayer, or to give a brief statement of devotion or encouragement. Feel free to adapt and offer the material in this book.

You will discover that this book provides insight into definitions and usages for a number of Bible words that we often use readily in our society today, but not always with clear understanding or with the same meaning held by the Bible's writers. There is much to be gained by knowing what individual words in the Bible *mean*, and how that meaning may apply to today's world.

I encourage you to read these entries aloud. Your reading the Scriptures aloud will reinforce their content to your mind. Your reading aloud the "teaching" will cause both courage and inspiration to bubble inside you. Your reading aloud the prayer—with conviction—will be a way of putting your faith into action.

Let your children hear you pray these prayers. Pray them for your children and with your children. You will not only give them deep insight into how to build a relationship with God in prayer, but also give them insight into what the Word of God commands and means.

What you pray for yourself, pray for others. And what you pray for others, pray for yourself. In this way, you will strengthen your ties with other Christian believers everywhere!

And now for a challenge . . .

Consider sharing the availability of this book with your pastor, Sunday school teacher, or others in leadership at your church. Suggest that a group within your church begin an intentional, earnest commitment to put these prayers to work. The more members involved, mutually praying for one another, the better! Begin to pray for those who attend your church, as well as others in the greater community who might be drawn to your church. See what God will do!

2   PRAYERS WITH SCRIPTURES AND INSIGHTS

1

Spiritual Sensitivity

[Job said:]
God maketh my heart soft.
(Job 23:16 KJV)

A soft heart—often a heart made soft by an abundance of tears—is like soil softened by rain. It is a heart capable of receiving the seeds of new ideas, new compassion, new hope, and new understanding and receptivity toward God's mercy and His promise of an abundant life.

Lord, I pray today that Your beloved child will have a soft heart—a heart that flows with compassion towards others, a heart fully open to your leading, a heart that is truly spiritually sensitive to what You desire to do in his life and in the lives of all Your children. Let Your child see others as You see them, hear their cries as You hear them, and respond as Jesus would.

2

Fresh New Ideas

Let this mind be in you, which was also in Christ Jesus.
(Philippians 2:5 KJV)

What did Jesus think about? Very likely, the next thing God the Father wanted Him to do! That meant being open to new opportunities, new encounters, new methods, and new ways of expressing God's love, truth, and mercy. We are to follow Jesus' example and teaching. We are to be looking for the "new thing" that God has for us to do, and to be ready to meet the "new person" He is sending our way. Note, too, that we are made in the image of God the Father, the Creator of All. Every day is a day to be creative—and to be the person who says something new or establishes something new on the earth to bring God glory and honor.

Fill Your beloved child today with fresh, new ideas—ideas that give greater meaning to life, ideas that prompt creative ventures, ideas that bring about greater understanding. I pray that You, gracious Lord, will give Your child ideas that *work,* ideas that bring about good changes and produce reward. Give Your child ideas that have a seed of eternal benefit in them—ideas that point toward Heaven and that are for the benefit of all Your children, now and forever.

3

Wholeness

[The apostle Paul wrote:]
I pray God your whole spirit and soul and body be preserved blameless unto the coming of our Lord Jesus Christ.
(1 Thessalonians 5:23 KJV)

The Western "mind set" is prone to compartmentalization. Not so in the area where Jesus lived and the Gospel first took root. Every person was regarded as a "whole" entity, with spirit, soul (mind and emotions), and body inseparably and intricately intertwined. To be "blameless" in this verse means to be without sin, with all aspects of one's being functioning in perfect harmony with all other aspects. Wholeness is far more than mere physical health. It is health for the whole of a person, for the whole of life, and for the whole of God's purposes. We are never made perfectly whole quickly, or even in this lifetime. Wholeness is an ongoing process and the pursuit of wholeness is God-ordained for every person.

Father, help Your beloved one to be more and more open to Your healing, restorative, strengthening power. Make her more whole today than she was yesterday. Show her how to work with You to help create conditions that are ripe for greater wholeness tomorrow. Bring her to the fullness of Your design for her life and make her whole.

> You will not stumble while on your knees.
>
> —Anonymous

4

Strength

Trust ye in the LORD forever: for in the LORD Jehovah is everlasting strength.
(Isaiah 26:4 KJV)

A person can do everything in his or her power to become "physically fit" and strong in muscle mass. But strength is more than physical. It takes strength in soul (mind and emotions), as well as spiritual strength, to do battle with *all* of life's problems and win! Emotional and spiritual strength is found fully in a relationship with God through Christ Jesus. There are no shortcuts to growing in this type of strength—the exercise requires ongoing bended knees, obedience, and humility.

Make Your beloved one strong today! As she trusts in you, O Lord, impart to her Your presence, which is all she will need to battle evil in all the areas of life: spiritual, physical, emotional, and mental. Let her *feel* Your strengthening presence, I pray.

5

Clear Thinking

God is not a God of confusion, but of peace.
(1 Corinthians 14:33 NAS)

True "peace of mind" comes when a person knows *what* to do, *how* to do it, and *when to do it*. There is a precision and a clarity to God's wisdom. Knowing God's plans and purposes is not a "guessing game." Neither are His plans and purposes a "hide and seek game." God desires to show you what He desires for you, as well as what He requires of you.

Help your servant, O Lord, to think clearly today—to see what *is*, to see what *should be*, and to see what *really matters* now and for eternity. Help him to find the answer to the besetting question, and the solution to the thorny problem. Help him to see with tremendous clarity *exactly* where You would have him walk, what You would have him say, and how You desire for him to act. Lift the cloud of confusion, Lord. Help Your beloved child to think as Jesus thinks.

6

Remembering What Needs to Be Remembered

Remember all the way which the Lord your God has led you . . . Remember the Lord your God.
(Deuteronomy 8:2,18 NAS)

Our memory has been given to us so we might repeat what is good and avoid repeating what is bad! God desires first and foremost that we remember *Him*—that we remember to make Him the central and foremost factor of every hour of a day. And, He desires that we remember how He has led us, tested us, humbled us, and examined us. The key to making good choices and decision in the future always depends, in part, on the degree to which we *actively* recall the lessons God has taught us in our past.

Give your beloved child an enhanced memory today—to recall Your Word, to recall the ways in which You have acted on her behalf in times past, and to recall Your prophetic promises. Help her to sort out her memories for greater understanding of Your purposes and plans. Help her remember what *needs* to be remembered to fulfill Your desires for her today.

7

Creativity

He has filled them with skill to perform every work of an engraver and of a designer and of an embroiderer, in blue and in purple and in scarlet material, and in fine linen, and of a weaver, as performers of every work and makers of designs.
(Exodus 35:35 NAS)

In addition to the craftsmanship described above, Moses noted that the artisans appointed to work on the tabernacle of God were good at stonework, wood carving, and metal work. He described them as capable of performing "every inventive work" (35:33) God does not desire any person's work be shoddy or ugly. Rather, He desires that the things we produce, in every area of our life, be "styled" in a way that is beautiful, harmonious, and worshipful.

Impart a burst of creativity, I pray, to Your child today so that he might apply full energy to a new idea, a new approach, a new concept, or a new venture. Inspire new art, new music, new awareness of beauty. You are the Creator—place today in Your beloved child a greater measure of Your creative power.

8

Perseverance

Be on the alert with all perseverance and petition for all the saints. (Ephesians 6:18 NAS)

We are to have enduring strength in all of our works aimed at justice, ministry, and the meeting of needs. The foremost areas of perseverance, however, must be in our "awareness" and our prayer. We are to be watchful at all times, *actively looking* for areas in which we can be the embodiment of Christ Jesus. We are to be in prayer *continuously*. Many people find it is far easier to endure at a physical task or an intellectual exercise than to remain CONSTANTLY on alert and in prayer.

Give your beloved child the power to persevere, O Lord. Help him to stand, and to keep on standing. Help him to believe, and keep on believing. Help him to persist in the pursuit of good with graciousness, but also with moral fiber like coated steel that does not break, does not bend, and does not rust. Assure him that You are standing with him, speaking through him, and upholding him in Your everlasting arms. Assure him that You will walk the full journey with him until victory is won.

> When everyone seemed panic-stricken, I got down on my knees before Almighty God and prayed. Soon a sweet comfort crept into my soul.
>
> — Abraham Lincoln

9

Finding What Has Been Lost

[Jesus taught,]
"What woman, if she has ten silver coins and loses one coin, does not light a lamp and sweep the house and search carefully until she finds it? When she has found it, she calls together her friends and neighbors, saying, 'Rejoice with me, for I have found the coin which I had lost!' In the same way, I tell you, there is joy in the presence of the angels of God over one sinner who repents."
(Luke 15:8–10 NAS)

Women in Bible times often wore a headband stitched with coins. Ten coins signified the woman was married. When this woman lost a coin, it reduced her headband to the status of an unmarried woman—in essence, she had lost her identity! No wonder this woman in Jesus' parable searched for her lost coin until she found it. There is nothing worse than losing your hope, your ability to love, or your identity.

Help your child today, O Lord, to find the thing of value that has been lost. Help her to recover the tradition that has disappeared. Her to reclaim the vibrancy of life that has become stale, and to reconcile the relationships that have gone awry. Help her to rediscover Your love and to rekindle her ability to love others. Help her to feel again Your near presence and renew to her the joy of salvation in Christ Jesus.

*A good man's prayers will from the
deepest dungeon climb heaven's height,
and bring a blessing down.*

—Joanna Baillie

10

A New Depth of Spiritual Maturity

... Until we all attain to the unity of the faith, and of the knowledge of the Son of God, to a mature man, to the measure of the stature which belongs to the fullness of Christ.
(Ephesians 4:13 NAS)

The body ages and matures without any intention on the part of a boy or girl. Not so with the development of those aspects that are on the inside of a person. Our intellect, emotions, and spirit are all intended to *mature* as the result of things we do, and without any regard for a particular timetable. Interior maturity is better "sooner" rather than "later." The greatest challenge to maturity lies in the spiritual realm. The good news is that we have God's Word telling us the disciplines to pursue, the example of Jesus as our role model for maturity, and the help of those God sets in the Church for our help: apostles, prophets, evangelists, pastors, and teachers. (See Ephesians 4:11.) We are wise to avail ourselves of all resources and to GROW UP spiritually as quickly as we can.

Gently stretch Your beloved child today so that she might be ever-more conformed to the full character likeness of Your Son, Jesus Christ. Impart new insights into Your Word. Enlarge her capacity to give and receive love. Give new opportunities to make godly choices and decisions, and to give godly help to people in need. Give new awareness of Your presence and the flow of Your power within her. Give her a glimpse of what she *can* be according to Your plans and purposes.

> Prayer is a sincere, sensible,
> affectionate pouring out of the soul to
> God, through Christ, in the strength
> and assistance of the Spirit.
>
> —John Bunyan

11

Becoming More Christ-like

We are to grow up in all aspects into Him who is the head, even Christ.
(Ephesians 4:15 NAS)

We are wise to ask three questions when we encounter a problem, need, or challenge: What would Jesus THINK about this? What would Jesus SAY about this? What would Jesus DO about this? As we answer the questions, based upon the truth of God's Word, we should remain mindful about what it is that Jesus accomplished — those things that ONLY He could do, has done, and is still doing — and also what Jesus role-modeled with the intention that we follow His example. We grow spiritually when we *actively desire* to become more like Jesus every day and invite the Holy Spirit to show us how to be more like Him.

Help your beloved child to become more like Jesus today, and less like the enemy of her soul. Guide her into all things—all right thoughts, all right responses, all right circumstances—that will produce in her the character nature of Jesus. Help her to be ever more loving, joyful, patient, kind, merciful, self-controlled, faithful, peaceful, and humble before You and toward others.

12

Greater Compassion

Thou, O Lord, art a God full of compassion, and gracious, longsuffering, and plenteous in mercy and truth.
(Psalm 86:15 KJV)

Compassion moves a person away from unproductive sympathy toward active empathy. Compassion compels a person to seek justice for the oppressed, to rescue those in danger, and to bring solutions to those in need. Compassion is one of the most noble of virtues; it is designed to be a constant perspective and motivating force for the person who follows Jesus.

Increase, O Lord, compassion in your beloved child. Call him away from cynicism and criticism, and toward love and mercy.

13

Taking Full Advantage of All God-Given Opportunities

And a vision appeared to Paul in the night. A man of Macedonia stood and pleaded with him, saying, "Come over to Macedonia and help us." Now after he had seen the vision, immediately we sought to go to Macedonia, concluding that the Lord had called us to preach the gospel to them.
(Acts 16:9–10 NKJV)

The apostle Paul and his traveling companion Timothy had been to Phrygia and the region of Galatia, intent on preaching the word throughout Asia Minor. They then felt that the Holy Spirit was stopping them as they prepared to go to Bithynia. They bypassed Mysia traveling to Troas. It was there that Paul had a vision that directed him away from Asia and toward Europe. If you consult a map, you will see that God's plan was one hundred and eighty degrees opposite Paul's plan! We must always be on the alert for the opportunities that are obviously sent by *God*. In our pursuing and taking full advantage of those opportunities we experience true success!

Give insight, O Lord, into the opportunities that lie ahead. Rekindle hope. And give direction, I pray, for wisdom to take full advantage of all opportunities that are part of Your plan and purpose for the life of Your beloved one.

> *Prayer that begins with trustfulness,*
> *and passes on into waiting, will always*
> *end in thankfulness, triumph, and praise.*
>
> —Alexander Maclaren

14

Weighing All Options

[Jesus said,]
"When He, the Spirit of truth, has come, He will guide you into all truth."
(John 16:13 NKJV)

Jesus went on to say after the statement above that the Spirit would speak of things to come, He would glorify Christ Jesus, and He would take what is Christ's and declare it to us. What is Christ's? The one abiding and ongoing attribute of Christ Jesus is that He heals us and brings us to wholeness. It is the Spirit, therefore, that reveals to us the next steps we are to take that will glorify Christ and bring ourselves and others closer to a state of wholeness. Many options are available to every person every day. Only the Spirit can reveal the best option to pursue. Ask the Spirit to help you weigh all the options before you and to choose the one He calls *His* choice.

Help Your child today, Heavenly Father, to hear the Spirit's voice and to experience divine guidance for every hour, in every choice and decision, to bring glory to You and to be an agent of healing on this earth.

15

Boldness in Speaking about Jesus

"And now, Lord, take note of their threats, and grant that Your bond-servants may speak Your word with all confidence. . . . And with great power the apostles were giving testimony to the resurrection of the Lord Jesus, and abundant grace was upon them all.
(Acts 4:29, 33 NAS)

When Peter and John were detained by the religious authorities of their day, they were admonished not to speak or teach in the name of Jesus. They responded, "We cannot stop speaking about what we have seen and heard." After they were released and told other Christians in Jerusalem about their experience, they prayed for boldness—courage and confidence—to continue speaking about Jesus. They didn't back away from the threats, but rather, forged ahead in the Spirit!

Precious Lord, give Your child *boldness* to speak about You more and more! Give her opportunities today to give testimony to Your love and saving grace.

16

Letting Go of what Needs to Be Released

Let us lay aside every weight, and the sin which doth so easily beset us, and let us run with patience the race that is set before us.
(Hebrew 12:1 KJV)

The main Jewish position of prayer is standing, with hands raised at the elbows, open palms toward God. It is a stance that say, "I have nothing to hide and nothing of my own to hold." It is a position that welcomes God to place into the person's hands, and life, all that He desires. It is a position that is ready for walking, or running, toward God's established goals and outstretched everlasting arms.

Father, help Your beloved one to lay aside any thought or anxiety that is holding her back from pursuing the work You have designed for her. Help her to approach her God-ordained race with full energy and strength, keeping her eyes on Your goals and off earthly distractions. Give her both a desire and an ability to lay aside every sinful impulse and to lay aside every "weight of the world" that is pressing on her mind. Give her freedom to run!

> There are moments when whatever be the attitude of the body, the soul is on its knees.
>
> —Victor Hugo

17

Holding on to What Should Remain

Abhor what is evil. Cling to what is good.
(Romans 12:9 NKJV)

Most people have a fairly well-developed sense of right and wrong. The problem is not in *knowing* what we should do or not do, but in *wanting to do* the right thing. Human beings seems to enjoy dabbling in a little evil when they think they can get away with it. The problem is, a "little evil" damages the whole of our lives—like a black ink spot on a white suit, or like too much hot sauce in the soup. The apostle Paul uses a very strong word about the response to evil that God desires: *abhor* it. All of our effort should be focused on clinging to what is good and right before the Lord.

Help Your child, today, O Lord, to come to the point of *detesting* all that is evil. Give him the ability to discern good, and then to cling to it in thought, word, and deed.

18

Knowing When and What Things Need to Be Changed

[The Lord was pleased with Solomon's prayer:]
"Give your servant an understanding heart to judge Your people to discern between good and evil."
(1 Kings 3:9 NAS)

Discernment—often called an understanding heart in the Bible—gives a person the ability to judge between good and evil, and to then make choices about what to DO. We are never to accommodate or harbor evil; situations that are evil need to be changed, people who are evil need to be won to Christ or removed from our presence, and habits that produce anything other than wholeness and right relationship with God need to be "put away" from our lives. We must be diligent in asking God what changes in our lives *He* desires, and then as He reveals them to us, we must be diligent to make those changes. Timing is often critical to effective change. Just as we ask the Lord *what* He wants to edit, amend, establish, or remove from our lives, we are wise to ask Him *when* and *how*. His methods for change nearly always begin with prayer.

Reveal to Your beloved one the changes that You desire in his life, O Lord. Show him the situations that need justice, the habits that need altering, and the people who should be removed from his association. Show him what, when, and how.

19

Good Management of Resources

[Jesus said:]
"Render to Caesar the things that are Caesar's, and to God the things that are Gods."
(Mark 12:17 KJV)

Everything that we posses has been given to us by God. We may *think* we have earned material wealth or that we have inherited material possessions, but in truth, we only have what we have because God has enabled our earning, and has allowed us to have what we have. Stewardship of our resources boils down to what we give, what we save, and what we spend. God requires a certain level of giving from each of us. Man's wisdom tells us that we should save a portion of what we earn, and our "lust for stuff" often drives what we spend. Ultimately, all things have come from God, and all things are owing to Him, including accountability for what we think we should save and what we desire to spend.

Help Your child today, O heavenly Father, to be a good manager of all that You have put into her hand.

20

Good Management of Time

See then that you walk circumspectly, not as fools but as wise, redeeming the time, because the days are evil.
(Ephesians 5:15 NKJV)

Time is our greatest gift from God. He gives us ample time to do His bidding and fulfill our purpose in life. But, He does not give us "extra" time to squander on our own whims and wishes. To "redeem" something, in this context, is to fulfill a pledge or promise. In this case, it is the pledge or promise God has given to us that we are His people, set on this earth to do His bidding and accomplish His goals. We are to walk circumspectly, which means to weigh all risks and consequences and refuse to act before taking into consideration all known potential outcomes. And once we know the right "way" to walk, we must be diligent in doing what God has set before us to do. We must not compromise with the world, nor are we to compromise God's plans and purposes with our own self-centered and manmade ideas and goals. Our job is to fulfill the promise God has placed within us.

Lord, help Your beloved child today to walk wisely and to work diligently. There's no time to waste in doing Your bidding!

The fewer words the better prayer.

—Martin Luther

21

Good Nutrition

Daniel said to the overseer whom the commander of the officials had appointed over Daniel, Hananiah, Mishael, and Azariah, "Please test your servants for ten days, and let us be given some vegetables to eat and water to drink."
(Daniel 1:11–12 NAS)

Even though they had been transported as captive to Babylon, Daniel and his close friends knew that the Lord still required them to be faithful to the Law of Moses, including the laws forbidding Babylonian delicacies and wine. They chose to eat the way God had instructed them to eat, rather than to eat the "finest" that the world had to offer them. We are wise when we, too, choose to eat according to biblical principles. The experts in nutrition tells us today that the Mediterranean diet—loaded in fruits, whole grains, and vegetables, with very little meat—is an extremely healthful way to eat. That is the way Jesus ate, and it still works for health today.

Give Your servant wisdom, O Lord, about what to eat, and what not to eat—in good balance, in right quantity, and on a schedule that produces maximum health benefits.

22

Knowing What to Say to Critics

[Jesus said,]
"When they bring you before the synagogues and the rulers and the authorities, do not worry about how or what you are to speak in your defense, or what you are to say; for the Holy Spirit will teach you in that very hour what you ought to say."
(Luke 12:11–12 NAS)

Every Christian is falsely criticized, accused, or persecuted at some point. The challenge is how to respond! Jesus said we should be aware that a defense of our faith will be required, but that we should not be concerned with *precisely* what we are to say. Every situation is different and there is no dress rehearsal for crisis moments. Rather, we are to trust the Holy Spirit to reveal to us what to say, which examples and experiences we are to share, what evidence from Scripture we are to give, and what lines of argument we might use for *precisely* those who are accusing us. The only preparation is to KNOW JESUS and to KNOW the WORD OF GOD.

Help Your servant, Father, to know You so well that she will be able to hear Your Holy Spirit whispering in her spirit what she is to say to those who accuse or persecute her for her faith. Help her not to rely on her own wit or intellect, but on what it is that You know will reach deep into the heart of the person who is oppressing her.

23

Strength to Replace Insecurity and Weakness

Hear my cry, O God:
Give heed to my prayer.
(Psalm 61:1 NAS)

The psalmist cries to God. "From the end of the earth I call to You when my heart is faint: lead me to the rock that is higher than I. For You have been a refuge for me, a tower of strength against the enemy." (vs. 2-3) Anytime we are feeling insecure or weak, we do well to 1) cry to the Lord, 2) recall His past refuge and strength, and 3) directly request that He *lead* us to the place of strength that He has already prepared for us.

Assure Your beloved one O Lord, of Your presence and Your guidance. Remind him of your past protection and provisions. Show him specifically what his next step should be. Strengthen him on the inside so he will be prepared to take full advantage of the opportunities that You will present to him.

24

Knowing When to Keep Quiet

The high priest stood up and said to Him, "Do you not answer? What is it that these men are testifying against You?" But Jesus kept silent. (Matthew 26:62–63 NAS)

After Jesus was arrested in the Garden of Gethsemane, he was taken to the High Priest and there, witnesses accused Him of saying He would destroy the Temple and rebuild it in three days. Jesus refused to engage in any discussion of that type—it was blatantly untrue and any acknowledgement of the charge would have been to give some credence to it. Jesus did not reply. When the high priest next said, "Tell us whether You are the Christ, the Son of God," Jesus readily answered! He said, "You have said it yourself; nevertheless I tell you, hereafter you will see the SON OF MAN SITTING AT THE RIGHT HAND OF POWER, and COMING IN THE CLOUDS OF HEAVEN." (vs. 64) Not every charge against you needs to be justified or answered. There are times to speak up, and times to remain silent.

Give Your child wisdom, O Lord, about when to stay silent and when to speak up. Don't let her become entangled in arguments or discussions that are rooted in lies. Give her boldness to speak up in discussions that are rooted in truth.

25

A Desire for Holiness

[The apostle Paul wrote:]
Let us cleanse ourselves from all defilement of flesh and spirit, perfecting holiness in the fear of God.
(2 Corinthians 7:1 NAS)

Holiness is not a synonym for goodness. The word "holiness" refers to being "separated," and specifically, "set apart for God's purposes." God is holy because He is "other"—He is in an entirely separate category from man. The followers of Jesus are called to be "separate"—or holy—in relationship to the world. We are to live without any defilement, corruption, or evil pollutants, both in the natural realm and the spiritual realm.

Give Your child a deep desire for holiness, Lord. Let her quickly say "no" to anything that would defile her physically or spiritually. Give her a hunger to be more and more like You.

> Men may spurn our appeals, reject our message, oppose our arguments, despise our persons, but they are helpless against our prayer.
>
> —Sidlow Baxter

26

A Desire to Serve

Paul, a bond-servant of God and an apostle of Jesus Christ, for the faith of those chosen of God and the knowledge of the truth which is according to godliness.
(Titus 1:1 NAS)

The apostle Paul was quick to call himself a bond-servant—a slave—totally owned by Christ Jesus for whatever purposes Christ might have for him. It was Paul's submission as a servant to Christ that allowed him to be effective as a servant to lost and suffering humanity. Jesus said, "Whoever wishes to become great among you shall be your servant; and whoever wishes to be first among you shall be slave of all." (See Mark 4:43–44 NAS.) Paul also knew the *purpose* of his service: it was for the faith of those chosen of God. It was for the impartation of truth that produces godliness. What a wonderful thing to know the One you serve, and why He has called you to service!

Give Your child, O Lord, the heart of a willing and obedient servant. Show her the precise areas in which You desire for her to serve.

27

More of the Holy Spirit Manifested in Daily Life

As the Lord has assigned to each one, as God has called each, in this manner let him walk.
(1 Corinthians 7:17 NAS)

Jesus sent the Holy Spirit to be our Comforter, manifesting God's love and mercy toward us. He also said the Holy Spirit would be our

Counselor, revealing to us not only the truth of Christ Jesus, but also the true way in which we are to walk. Every hour of every day, we NEED the Holy Spirit's direction and abiding presence. It is the Holy Spirit who knows fully the path assigned to each one of us, and the call of God on our lives as we walk that path. Our journey includes other people, and thus, a major part of our "assignment" and "call" of God will always be related to those with whom we are in relationship. Ask God daily WHAT you are to do and where you are to go, and HOW you are to give witness to Christ and express God's love as you encounter others and face life's challenges.

Help Your beloved one to listen more closely to You, Holy Spirit. Give her guidance and then give her courage to walk out Your plan for her. Manifest Yourself to her daily so that she might manifest You in all that she says and does.

28

A Good Medical Report

As He entered a village, ten leprous men who stood at a distance met Him; and they raised their voices, saying, "Jesus, Master, have mercy on us!" When He saw them, He said to them, "Go and show yourselves to the priests." And as they were going they were cleansed.
(Luke 17:12–14 NAS)

The priests in Bible times were the ones who diagnosed leprosy (according to rules established in the Law of Moses), and they were also the ones who pronounced that leprosy had been healed. Those who were deemed to be lepers were required to live apart from society and to have no contact with those who did not have the disease. Jesus clearly spoke in a way that both imparted faith and healing to this band of lepers, but He also sent them to the "medical authorities" of His day for confirmation that they had been healed and could be restored to their families and friends. Jesus did not dismiss the need for medical documentation or verification. He knew that a true miracle always stands up to close analysis!

Assure Your child, Heavenly Father, that You are her healer, and also that You use doctors and medicines as instruments that are ultimately in Your hand. Give her an eagerness to confirm the healing work that You are doing in her life, and also to confirm the good health that You are imparting to her daily.

29

New Insights into Holy Scripture

Behold, I long for Your precepts.
(Psalm 119:40 NAS)

Psalm 119 is all about the Word of God and the psalmist's desire to know it better, to develop a deeper relationship with the Lord, and to be more fully equipped to obey the commands of the Lord. Every time we open the Bible to read it, we are wise to ask God to help us remember what we read, to see ways to apply what we read, and to gain new insights into the nature and character of God as we read. God delights in revealing more of Himself to those who delight in knowing Him!

Give Your child, O Lord, a deeper desire to read Your Word. Give her new insights into who You are, what You command and promise, and how You desire for her to live each day.

> *"Christian! seek not yet repose." Hear*
> *thy guardian angel say: Thou art in the*
> *midst of foes—"Watch and pray."*
>
> —Charlotte Eliott

30

An Insatiable Hunger and Thirst for Righteousness

[Jesus said:]
"Blessed are those who hunger and thirst for righteousness, for they shall be satisfied."
(Matthew 5:6 NAS)

We are to desire God's "right ways" of living as our most basic need! Just as a person cannot live for long without food and water, so we *must* know God's desires for us and live them out if we are truly to be satiated and fulfilled in life.

Impart to your beloved child a deep desire to "do the right thing"—as You, O Lord, define "right." Give her a desire to stay as far away from evil as possible, never flirting with it or tempting God. Satisfy her hunger and thirst for You and Your commandments, I pray, with your wisdom and clear direction.

31

A Contrite Heart

For thus says the high and exalted One Who lives forever, whose name is Holy, "I dwell on a high and holy place. And also with the contrite and lowly of spirit in order to revive the spirit of the lowly and to revive the heart of the contrite."
(Isaiah 57:15 NAB)

The contrite person is truly and deeply sorry for his sins; he has a strong sense of remorse or guilt, and feels ashamed, usually with an accompanying determination not to sin again. The "lowly in spirit" is a person who sees himself in proper perspective before God—to be "lowly in spirit" has nothing to do with a comparison to other human beings. Neither does it have to do with self-worth or self-esteem. The person lowly in spirit KNOWS that he isn't in charge of all things, God is; he doesn't know all things, God does; he can't do everything, but God can; he is created, and God alone is the Creator. The prophet points out clearly that God is under no obligation to dwell in relationship with man—rather, He *chooses* to do so in order to revive us spiritually so we might confess our sins to Him, be forgiven of them, and enjoy a fully reconciled relationship and ever-deepening friendship with our heavenly Father.

Give Your servant a contrite heart today, dear Father. Give her such intense sorrow for her sins that she will want to *run* to You for forgiveness and restoration!

32

Greater Humility

Humble yourselves in the presence of the Lord, and He will exalt you.
(James 4:10 NAS)

Humility is not making yourself a doormat so that others might walk on you or step over you in pursuit of their own goals. Rather, it is falling on one's face—figuratively—before God, allowing God to lift you up in His own timing and by His own methods to use you for His purposes to bring Him greater glory. Humility is the *attitude* that accompanies acts of total submission to God's will.

I pray today that You, O Heavenly Father, will give Your beloved child a willingness to submit totally to Your will. Give him a heart that is humble before You.

33

God's Wisdom

Let the word of Christ dwell in you richly in all wisdom, teaching and admonishing one another in psalms and hymns and spiritual songs, singing with grace in your hearts to the Lord.
(Colossians 3:16 NKJV)

Wisdom is not for the individual believer alone. It is for the *BODY* of Christ as a whole. What you learn of God and from God—through study of His Word and an ongoing and deepening relationship with Him—is intended to be shared with others, in teachings, words of admonition, and through songs of praise, songs of declaration, and creative songs of the Spirit. What we share must be shared with the mercy, love, and goodwill of God (His grace) as our motivation and attitude. Much truth can be conveyed in a way that makes it easy to receive if that truth is presented with a melody!

As You reveal Yourself to Your beloved child, O Lord, I pray that you will give Your child opportunities to share those insights with others—imparting wisdom in every avenue of communication possible and with an attitude of Your generous love and mercy. Let the Word of God not only enrich her life, but the lives of all around her.

34

A Reversal of the Negative

[The Lord said through Moses:]
"If you are unfaithful I will scatter you among the peoples; but if you return to Me and keep My commandments and do them, though those of you who have been scattered were in the most remote part

of the heavens, I will gather them from there and bring them to the place where I have chosen to cause My name to dwell."
(Nehemiah 1:8–9 NASB)

God calls a situation "negative" if His people are unfaithful and in disobedience, and therefore, become scattered among the wicked of the world. The reversal of that situation requires a return to the Lord and obedience to His commandments. Virtually any situation we might call "negative" can be traced directly to an act of disobedience, even those situations in which the person being injured is *not* directly unfaithful. We often are the "victims" of consequences meted out to convict others of their sin. The demand on the innocent is to remain faithful and obedient, and to encourage others to return to the Lord in genuine repentance.

Only You, O Lord, know how to turn a negative situation into a positive. Only You know the best methods to use in the best timing. Only You can see the end from the beginning. I pray today that You will be the author of both a second chance and a transformed spirit.

35

Ongoing Growth and Development

Blessed are they that dwell in thy house . . .
Blessed is the man whose strength is in thee . . .
They go from strength to strength.
(Psalm 84:4–5, 7 KJV)

In every area of our life, God desires that we go from our current position to a stronger position. This is true for our physical development; it is true for our ongoing learning of information, gaining of understanding, and applying of wisdom. It is certainly true in our development of character and our ongoing spiritual growth—from conversion through transformation and renewal, to a full expression of the maturity of Christ Jesus. We must never assume that we have "arrived" or that we have gained all that Christ desires to impart to us, or do through us.

Give Your child a desire to keep going and keep growing, O Lord. Show her how to turn weaknesses and faults into strengths, and how to turn strengths into even greater strengths.

36

A Greater Desire to Pray

In every thing by prayer and supplication with thanksgiving let your requests be made known unto God. And the peace of God, which passeth all understanding, shall keep your hearts and minds through Christ Jesus.
(Philippians 4:6–7 KJV)

Every person wants peace, both inner peace and outer peace with others. Peace, however, is not the absence of conflict as much as it is the abiding presence of God! How do we get this kind of peace—a peace that isn't rooted solely in the rational thinking of peaceful thoughts, or by making a reasonable decision to have peace? We have peace as a byproduct of trusting God in all things, and actively voicing that trust as a petition to Him. Our petitions, or requests, are to be made with thanksgiving that God has always taken care of us, is caring for us now, and will take care of us in the future.

Give Your child a greater desire to pray today as a means of experiencing greater peace in her heart. Show her the link between her experiencing inner peace and her voicing all of her requests to You, with thanksgiving.

37

Renewed Expressions of Gratitude

The ministry of this service is not only fully supplying the needs of the saints, but is also overflowing through many thanksgiving to God.
(2 Corinthians 9:12 NAS)

The apostle Paul was quick to point out to the believers in the first century church at Corinth that the gifts they made for his support and ongoing ministry not only met needs throughout the Body of Christ as a whole, but there financial gifts were producing ongoing expressions of thanks to God. The truth is: what we *do* for fellow believers not only helps them personally, but our giving becomes the sweet savor of a sacrifice rising to God. Our gifts take on a perspective of eternity when our thanks and praise are voiced to God, and the needs we meet result in the salvation of souls. Any time we do something in the name of Christ, we should begin to thank God for giving us the opportunity to serve Him and others, for producing the harvest of His desire in us and through us, and for helping us to proclaim His glory on this earth. We can never run out of things for which to thank God—not in this life or in eternity!

Give Your servant a quick desire to thank You more, not only for all You are doing on Your servant's behalf, but all You are doing *through* Your servant for others and for the cause of Christ. Give her a renewed awareness that her life counts! Give her a rekindled desire to voice gratitude to You in all things and for all things.

> *God's giving is inseparably connected with our asking.*
>
> —John Bunyan

38

More Spontaneous Thanks and Praise

Let us continually offer up a sacrifice of praise to God, that is, the fruit of lips that give thanks to His name.
(Hebrews 13:15 NAS)

Thanksgiving is related to the acts of God—what God has done in the past, is doing, or has promised to do (which is what God *will* do). The acts of God involve God's work in the lives of others, now and throughout the ages past. In contrast, praise is related to the unchanging everlasting nature of God—who God is, now and forever. You can never run out of things for which to thank God. New blessings occur minute by minute! You can never run out of things to praise God for—His nature is infinite in every facet of His being.

Give Your child, O Lord, a heart overflowing with thanksgiving and praise. Let him voice his thanks and praise spontaneously, frequently, and with great joy! Use his voicing of thanks and praise to refresh his spirit, and to renew hope, kindle faith, and expand love in him.

39

Greater Intentionality

I have set the LORD always before me.
(Psalm 16:8 NKJV)

To be intentional means to be purposeful. Intentionality involves advance thinking, or "forethought." It involves evaluation and active decision-making. It means taking into consideration *God's* opinions,

God's methods, and *God's* purposes before making choices or taking action. To be intentional means to do things "on purpose"—make that, "on GOD'S purpose."

Lord, give Your beloved one pause to "think things through" from Your viewpoint and to make choices and decisions that are truly ON PURPOSE—that fulfill purpose, pursue purpose, and are based on Your truth.

40

A Renewed Sense of Purpose

[The Lord said through the prophet Jeremiah:]
"Who is like Me? Who will arraign Me?
And who is that shepherd who will withstand Me?"
Therefore hear the counsel of the LORD . . .
And His purposes that He has purposed.
(Jeremiah 49:19–20 NKJV)

God has a plan and purpose for EVERYTHING. Nothing happens by coincidence or happenstance. His plans and purposes are intricate, involving every person at all times. We must understand that God has a timely and everlasting PURPOSE before we attempt to discern our role in His plan, which then becomes OUR purpose, both for today and for eternity.

Help, O Lord, Your beloved one to have renewed discernment into what it is that YOU are seeking to do on the earth—right now. Give her insight into how her life fits into Your plan and show her how she can fulfill her purpose in life by embedding her life and all of her purpose in You.

Prayer is invading the impossible.

—Jack Hayford

41

Godly Understanding

[The apostle Paul expressed this desire for the Colossians:]
"Attaining to all the wealth that comes from the full assurance of understanding, resulting in a true knowledge of God's mystery, that is, Christ Himself, in whom are hidden all the treasures of wisdom and knowledge."
(Colossians 2:2–3 NASB)

Understanding goes beyond the acquisition of knowledge. Understanding involves insight into God's timing, God's methods, and always, God's purposes. No person can ever answer all of the "why" questions in life. But every believer can know the One who has all the answers! Does this lead to blind trust of God? No. It leads to eyes-wide-open and eager-to-learn trust in God!

I pray today, O Lord, that You will bestow more understanding on our beloved child. Reveal more about Your plans and purposes. Reveal more about the ways in which Jesus fulfilled His mission on this earth. Reveal more about Your great love.

42

A Willingness to Be Trained

[Jesus taught:]
"Blessed are the meek,
For they shall inherit the earth."
(Matthew 5:5 NKJV)

The Bible word for a trainable spirit is meekness. In ancient England, the word "meek" was used to describe a horse that had been trained to respond quickly to bit and bridle—such a horse was most useful to its rider, in both peacetime and war. The Lord desires that His people be humble, pliable, and quickly responsive to His bidding so they might be in the best possible position to say and do those things that rebuke evil and bring rewards of all kind.

Help Your child, O heavenly Father, to be willing to be "bridled" for Your purposes. Help her to be totally responsive to Your Spirit speaking within her so that You might use her fully in Your plans and purposes.

43

Discipline

Whatever your hand finds to do, do it with your might.
(Ecclesiastes 9:10 NKJV)

God sends us work. It is not happenstance that we "find" a job or are asked to do an important task. All things are under God's control, even if we are unaware of His engineering those things that come our way as "work." Our part in the process is to discipline our lives so that we accomplish God's work with tight focus and full energy. Discipline always implies order and a maintenance of self-control even in times that are difficult, stressful, or changing.

Lord, help Your child today to discipline her life to accomplish all that You have set before her to do.

Praying without faith is like trying to cut with a blunt knife—much labour expended to little purpose.

—James O. Fraser

44

An Eagerness to Learn More

Teach me, O LORD, the way of Your statutes, and I will keep it to the end.
(Psalm 119:33 NKJV)

The psalmist was eager to learn the WAY associated with God's law—the word "way" not only refers to direction, but to all details related to methods and timing. When we know precisely what God is directing us to do and when, we then must be committed to walking out His way, eagerly looking for others who will walk out His way with us.

Reveal to Your child, Lord, how he might stay in step with Your plan, Your timing, and Your methods. Help Your beloved one to follow in Your footsteps every day of his life.

45

Greater Kindness Displayed toward Others

Be kind to one another, tenderhearted, forgiving one another, even as God in Christ forgave you.
(Ephesians 4:32 NKJV)

Kind. Tenderhearted. Forgiving. These are the "top three" manifestations of God's love and grace in the life of a believer. They are also to be the hallmarks of our behavior toward others. We all want to be treated with kindness, tenderness, and to be forgiven for our faults and trespasses. In turn, we usually find that a person who is kind, tenderhearted, and forgiving is irresistible. Such people reflect the mercy of God. They point to the truth of God's love and free offer of forgiveness to all who will turn to Him.

Help Your beloved child today to display Your kindness and tenderness to others, freely forgiving even as she seeks forgiveness.

46

Greater Extending of God's Mercy

[Jesus taught:]
"Be merciful, just as your Father is merciful."
(Luke 6:36 NAS)

Another word for "merciful" is compassionate. The compassionate person seeks to put an end to distress, oppression, or injustice. Compassion goes beyond feelings of sympathy to take *action* to resolve a need, problem, or difficulty. The mercy of God encompasses God's love and forgiveness. In truth, the most compassionate thing we can ever do for another person is to point them toward God's mercy. God's forgiveness is balm that relieves all types of distress!

Gracious and loving Lord, reveal to Your child opportunities to be merciful and compassionate today.

47

Greater Peace

Thou wilt keep him in perfect peace, whose mind is stayed on thee: because he trusteth in thee.
(Isaiah 26:3 KJV)

A "perfect peace" is a peace that contributes to wholeness. Wholeness encompasses a complete harmony between man and God, good relationships with other believers, and an internal harmony of spirit, mind, and emotions within a person. The only way to experience that kind of peace—which the apostle Paul called a peace *beyond* understanding—is to immerse one's self into a totally reconciled, submitted, and obedient relationship with our loving Heavenly Father. No matter what the circumstances might be, trust in God sends a message to yourself and all around you, "God is in control, and therefore, blessing lies ahead!"

Pour out Your peace today into the heart of Your child, Heavenly Father. Help her to trust You more and to stay focused on what You know and can do about every situation that is troublesome to her.

48

More Joy

[The angel said in announcing Jesus' birth:]
"Behold, I bring you good news of great joy which will be for all the people."
(Luke 2:10 NAS)

Joy is not something directly attained by either a manipulation of circumstances, the acquisition of information, or a resolute decision to have more joy. Rather, joy is an inner working of the Spirit that is a by-product of a person's commitment to Christ Jesus, expressions of love for God and others, and the hope of eternal life and eternal reward. The more we focus our lives on these "prerequisites," the more we WANT to voice thanks and praise. Praise and thanksgiving tap into the wellspring of joy that has been created by our love, hope, and faith. In turn, it renews that wellspring! The process is cyclical—the more we have joy, the more we express thanks and praise, and the more our joy is renewed.

Give your servant, O Lord, an increased capacity for joy. Show him what it really means to follow Christ, to love others, and to use his faith. Show him how much You love him. Pour Your joy into him as he gives thanks and praise to You for all You have done and all that You are. Don't let him settle for mere happiness that is rooted in circumstance. Give him a taste of Your joy that will truly satisfy and strengthen him.

49

Greater Quickness to Resolve Adversarial Relationships

[Jesus said:]
"Make friends quickly with your opponent at law while you are with him in the way, so that your opponent may not hand you over to the judge, and the judge to the officer, and you be thrown in prison." (Matthew 5:25 NAS)

Prison in Jesus' time was nearly always a "debtors" prison—people were imprisoned to work and then, from their earnings, to compensate those they had wronged. Their "upkeep" in prison fell to family members, who were required to provide for all of their food, clothing, and bedding needs. Jesus taught that reconciliation with our enemies or opponents, including those we have "treated" as enemies in our trespasses against them, is *our* responsibility. We are far wiser to seek a mediated solution than to face a lawsuit. If we have wronged another person, we must seek to make amends, and we are wise to do it in a way that brings about satisfaction to the one we have wronged. If we have not wronged another person, but the other person believes we have, we are still wise to seek reconciliation, rather than dismiss their accusations or claims. The truth is, a judge's decision is rarely going to be *entirely* in our favor, even if we are not at fault. At minimum, there will be attorney fees and court costs, as well as a load of stress and a waste of time!

Help Your child today, O Lord, to move quickly to admit fault and to seek to make amends with those she hurts or harms. Do not let adversarial feelings grow into bitterness or hatred. Show her that it is *wrong* to feel a need to be *right* in every situation, argument, or transaction.

50

Freedom from Tormenting Memories

[Jesus said:]
A woman, when she is in labor, has sorrow because her hour has come; but as soon as she has given birth to the child, she no longer remembers the anguish, for joy that a human being has been born into the world. Therefore you now have sorrow; but I will see you again and your heart will rejoice, and your joy no one will take from you."
(John 16:21–22 NKJV)

God has given us memory so we will not WANT to repeat those things that are evil or that bring us torment, and so we WILL remember and want to repeat those things that produce good or give us joy. God does NOT give us memories to torment us. If you suffer from tormenting memories, ask the Lord to free you from them and to replace the ideas that haunt you or fill your dreams with new ideas rooted in the joy and peace of His presence.

Free Your beloved one today, O gracious Father, from any tormenting memories. Show her that You have always loved her and been with her, and that You love her today and want only the best for her. Reveal to her Your desire to defeat the enemy on her behalf!

Prayer is not eloquence, but earnestness.

—Sir Thomas More

51

Restraining from Judgment and Condemnation

[Jesus said:]
"Judge not, and you shall not be judged. Condemn not, and you shall not be condemned."
(Luke 6:37 NKJV)

To "judge" is to evaluate a situation in order to render a decision related to it—usually a negative consequence or punishment. No person is in a position to render *decisions* related to what should happen to another person for their sins, failures, or shortcomings. Only God knows how their actions and His forgiveness might create a newness of life. When we judge others we take on a responsibility and privilege that is not ours—and that puts us into the error column as much as the person we have been judging! The same for condemnation, which is declaring that another person is not *worthy* of forgiveness or mercy. Those who make that severe pronouncement over others—in word or attitude—totally lose sight of their own need for forgiveness or mercy. Sin and forgiveness do not exist on a manmade "sliding scale." They are absolutes, and all absolutes fall into God's domain. We must leave all judgment and condemnation to Him!

Free Your child today, heavenly Father, from all judgment and condemnation of others. Help her to pray for mercy for others, even as she prays for mercy for herself!

> *God looks not at the oratory of your prayers, how elegant they may be . . . but the sincerity of them.*
>
> —Thomas Brooks

52

Asking for and Receiving God's Forgiveness

If we confess our sins, He is faithful and just to forgive us our sins and to cleanse us from all unrighteousness.
(1 John 1:9 NKJV)

There is no sin beyond God's ability to forgive it—which means setting us free from the eternal consequences of that sin, and restoring us to full relationship with God the Father. God's forgiveness "cleanses" us. His forgiveness fully removes the stain of guilt and shame. There is only one thing required to receive God's forgiveness—we must admit that we need it! We must confess that we have sinned and ask God to forgive us. He surely will!

Give Your child complete assurance today that when he comes to You asking for forgiveness, You *will* forgive. Give him a hunger for your total cleansing power for His mind and heart, O Lord.

53

Forgiving One's Own Self

If You, LORD, should mark iniquities,
O Lord, who could stand? But there is forgiveness with You,
That You may be feared.
(Psalm 130:3-4 NAS)

The Bible speaks of three "varieties" of sin—there is the "sin" that is rooted in rebellion and results in separation from God; there are "trespasses" against other people; and there are "iniquities," which are attitudes, beliefs, and behaviors rooted in us genetically and as a result of our fallen sin nature. Iniquities are often called the "iniquities of the fathers"—they are learned behaviors that become so ingrained in us that they seem to be our human "nature." God promises to free us from our "nature!" He desires to reverse multi-generational trends and patterns. We each have inherited a propensity to behave in certain ways; we have learned, apart from our own choosing, the sinful patterns of thinking and responding to life that previous generations in our family adopted. Ask God to set you free from these so you might be truly the person He desires you to be, unbound from all sinful influences and desires you may have "inherited." God did not cause or create your "iniquities." He desires to set you free from them! God also does not desire that you beat yourself up over your own failures and sins. Ask God to forgive you and then believe that He has done so! Choose to forgive yourself and burrow into His Word so you might learn how He desires for you to think, feel, and behave.

Free Your beloved child today, loving Lord, from the iniquities of previous generations and all cultural influences that promote sin and trespasses. Create in him a new mind and heart that reflects You.

54

Trusting God to Fill the Void

Do not hide Your face from me,
Do not turn Your servant away in anger;
You have been my help;
Do not abandon me nor forsake me,
O God of my salvation!
(Psalm 27:9 NAS)

Voids occur in our lives when we wall off certain areas from God. He fills all the voids He is allowed to fill! If we have a void in energy, creativity, wisdom, comfort, provision, protection, love, value—a void of *anything* that is part of what God has created and provided for us through Christ Jesus—we must turn to the Lord and pray as the psalmist prayed, "Do not abandon me nor forsake me." God has promised to be our salvation—and the root word in Hebrew is the same root word for the English words of salvation, healing, and wholeness. God desires to fill all the voids in your life, if you will only let Him!

Give Your servant today, O Father, a strong awareness that the true answer to all of her feelings of lack is this: More of You! Help her to turn to You with total trust that You are there, not only present, but able and willing to fill her with Your overcoming presence.

55

A Quiet Spirit

He who listens to me shall live securely
And will be at ease from the dread of evil.
(Proverbs 1:33 NAS)

Evil is usually obvious and nearly always requires a direct confrontation. The "dread" of evil is far more subtle. Dread is extreme fear, but with an added "reluctance" to do anything that a person perceives might be upsetting or have the potential to make a bad situation worse. God wants us to be totally secure in His ability to help us both withstand and overcome evil, and that includes all "dread." There is nothing to be feared—ultimately—in a situation that calls for standing up for what is right and true. God will regard our stance as an act of faith for the cause of righteousness, and that stance always brings God's reward, comfort, and an eternal benefit. Our fears are what keep us from living "securely."

Give Your child a desire to rise above all dread of evil, to confront what needs to be confronted, and to trust You with the consequences. Give her Your security today, loving Lord.

56

Sweet Sleep

When you lie down, your sleep will be sweet.
(Proverb 3:24b NAS)

Sweet sleep includes the ability to fall asleep, stay asleep, sleep long enough for genuine rejuvenation of one's body and mind, and to awaken refreshed and energetic. Sweet sleep is also marked by a lack of nightmares or troubling dreams. How does one attain sweet sleep? The previous verses in Proverbs give the key: "Keep sound wisdom and discretion." Doing this includes the admonitions to "turn away from all evil." Keep your mind focused on what is good and right before the Lord, and release all the day's worries and mistakes to Him! He can handle the world while you are asleep.

Give Your child sweet sleep, Lord. Help her to trust You completely, without worry or fear.

57

An Awareness and Appreciation of God's Grace

The grace of our Lord Jesus Christ be with your spirit.
(Galatians 6:18 NAS)

Grace is God's work in our lives—at God's initiative and totally apart from anything we can earn or deserve. God's work is always marked by love, mercy, favor, and goodwill. We must let these attributes of God's grace resonate in us—if we do not, we will tend to think of God only as a judge who seeks to control us and severely restrict us. In turn, when we fail to acknowledge the grace of God, with gratitude and praise, we are much more likely to seek to control others, rather than trust God to work directly, freely, and with "a warm welcome" in another person's life.

Lord, assure Your child today that the work You desire to do in him is a good work that will produce earthly blessing and eternal reward. Open his heart to receive Your grace.

58

Replacing a Bad Habit with a Good One

[The Lord said through the prophet Ezekiel:]
"When a wicked man turns away from his wickedness which he has committed and practices justice and righteousness, he will save his life."
(Ezekiel 18:27 NAS)

It is possible to turn from wickedness—to refrain from all patterns of evil thinking, false believing, and negative behaving. It *is* possible to begin to live in a way that promotes justice in our relationships with others and righteousness in our relationship with God. Note that the prophet refers to justice and righteousness as things we must *practice*. We need to be persistent in the *doing* of a new way of thinking and acting for it truly to become an instinctual habit. The move from wicked habits to godly ones is *our* responsibility. It is within God's free gift of free will for us to make attitudinal, emotional, and behavioral changes. The result is not eternal "salvation," but it is a "saving" of our earthly life—it promotes healing and wholeness, and puts us out of the direct path of incoming evil assault. When we ask God to give us His *power* to accompany our *will* to do what is right, He imparts true *willpower* to us!

> *Strength in prayer is better than length in prayer.*
>
> —Unknown

Help Your beloved servant today, gracious Father, to make an intentional and persistent choice to turn from wickedness, and to pursue justice and righteousness.

59

Deeper Friendships

There is a friend who sticks closer than a brother.
(Proverbs 18:24 NAS)

Friendships are desirable, but most of all, God desires to be our "foremost friend"—or in today's terms, our BFF (best friend forever). Jesus told His disciples the night before His crucifixion, "No longer do I call you slaves . . . but I have called you friends." (John 15:15) Friends are never perfect; they will always disappoint in some way at some time. But, deep and abiding friendships are possible, and loyal friends are God's gifts to us. Cherish your friends. Be a good friend. Forgive your friends freely and fully. BE the kind of friend you want to have.

I pray today, heavenly Father, that You will give Your beloved child just the right friends that he needs. Give him compassion for his friends. Let him cherish his friends and seek to be a faithful friend. Above all, dear Lord, reveal to him that YOU are the best friend he can ever have and ever need.

> *Prayer is always the BEST thing you can do . . . and the first thing you SHOULD DO . . . in any situation.*
>
> —J.L. Dargatz

60

A Renewed Mind

Do not be conformed to this world, but be transformed by the renewing of your mind, that you may prove what is that good and acceptable and perfect will of God.
(Romans 12:2 NKJV)

The apostle Paul encouraged the early church to pursue genuine spiritual renewal and transformation for three main purposes: l) know what is beneficial—especially producing wholeness (good), 2) know what is right before God (acceptable), and 3) know God's precise plans and purposes for the fulfillment of one's individual life. A mind that is not renewed by God—but is under the thought control of the world—cannot clearly know any of these three. Our first challenge is to turn away from the world as our source of opinion, and turn to God's Word.

Help Your child today, O Lord, to stay focused on what *You* desire and on what Your Word says. As she fills her mind with Your opinions, guide her into wholeness, obedience to Your commandments, and the fulfillment of her life purpose.

61

Genuine Reconciliation

[Jesus said:]
"First be reconciled to your brother, and then come and present your offering."
(Matthew 5:24 NAS)

Reconciliation is the mutual agreement to end a conflict, or a mutual decision to renew a friendship. Since reconciliation comes after a time of disagreement or rancor, mutual forgiveness is nearly always required. Both forgiveness and reconciliation have a prerequisite: a desire to move beyond personal pride to restore a mutuality of peace with another person. Jesus saw reconciliation as a necessity before a person might come before God and present an offering, expecting God's blessing and reward in response to his gift. One of the reasons all "gifts" might not bear a good harvest may very well be a lack of forgiveness and reconciliation!

Help Your child, O Lord, to confront any form of pride that keeps her from forgiving and seeking reconciliation with those who have wronged her. Help her to seek restoration of broken friendships and to offer a mutual agreement to end any estrangement, dispute, or adversarial relationship.

62

The Opportunity to Lead Someone to Christ Jesus

[Paul and Silas said:]
"Believe in the Lord Jesus, and you will be saved, you and your household." And they spoke the word of the Lord to him together with all who were in his house. And he took them that very hour of the night and washed their wounds, and immediately he was baptized, he and all his household.
(Acts 16:31–33 NAS)

Witnessing about Jesus is not nearly as complicated or frightening as many Christians seem to make it. We simply are to give others the opportunity to *believe and be saved*—to have their sins cleansed and to receive full reconciliation with God, now and forever. We must not fail to give the opportunity in as gracious and loving manner as possible. We must not feel rejected if the other person says "no" to Jesus. The Holy Spirit is the One who "seals" the deal when it comes to salvation; He alone knows the person's sincerity and motivation. Trust the Holy Spirit to lead you to a person who is open to receiving Christ, and then make the offer that truly can change their life forever!

Give Your child an opportunity to give witness to You today, precious Lord. Help her to boldly make the offer: "Believe and be saved."

63

An Opportunity to Tell Someone about God's Great Love

[Jesus said:]
"For God so loved the world that He gave His only begotten Son, that whoever believes in Him should not perish but have everlasting life."
(John 3:16 NKJV)

Jesus gave witness to God's great love. The message of God's love is the greatest message we can ever share with another person. Forgiveness of sin, and everlasting life, are embedded in God's love.

Gracious and loving Lord, send someone today to Your beloved one—a person who needs to hear that You are a God of love, mercy, and forgiveness. Give her boldness to share the truth of who You are and what You desire to do in the life of every person who makes the decision to believe in Christ Jesus.

> *God answers prayer in four main ways: yes, no, not now, and "I have something better."*
>
> —Anonymous

64

Taking Every Thought Captive

We are destroying speculations and every lofty thing raised up against the knowledge of God, and we are taking every thought captive to the obedience of Christ.
(2 Corinthians 10:5 NAS)

The apostle Paul noted two forms of thinking that are contrary to Christ's commands: 1) lofty ideas that are pride-filled and self-exalting, and 2) second-guessing about what God might do, as opposed to what Christ Jesus has said God *will* do. One type of thinking elevates and promotes self, the other presumes that man can know better than God what *should* be done in any given situation or circumstance. Thoughts such as these must be "taken captive"—recognized and conquered by the person thinking them!

Give Your grace today, dear Heavenly Father, to Your beloved servant so that he might recognize his self-exalting ideas and his speculations regarding Your choices and decisions. Help him to submit all of his thinking to Your will, in Your timing, according to Your methods, and always for Your purposes and glory forever!

65

Going a Second Mile

[Jesus said:]
"Whoever forces you to go one mile, go with him two."
(Matthew 5:41 NAS)

Nothing causes a person's anger or controlling impulses to dissipate faster than to do *more*—give more, extend more kindness —than the angry or demanding person requires. Jesus was referring specifically to the right of a Roman soldier to demand that a Jew under Roman occupation carry his burdens (backpack, belongings) for a mile. Jesus said, "Go for two!" You may not take the anger out of the person, but there is a good likelihood you will give the person no cause for venting an *increase* of anger toward you. In the end, you may be weary from the extra mile of burden carrying, but you are likely to be unwounded and alive to share the Gospel another day.

Give Your child a desire to go beyond the minimum demands and to excel in showing kindness and cooperation. Help, O Lord, Your beloved one to avoid negative consequences, injury, or verbal assault from those who seek to control her or use her.

66

Strong Spiritual Purpose for the Family

Except the LORD build the house, they labour in vain that build it. (Psalm 127:1 KJV)

In many areas of life, we must recognize that we are to do everything we *can* do, and then trust God to do what *only* He can do. Families are nearly always strengthened if all members of the family come to a consensus about *why* it is important for them to retain loyalty to the family, and why God molded them together as a family—in other words, the purposes for which their family was "created" by God This awareness of a divine purpose nearly always strengthens family ties.

Lord, please give your beloved child a glimpse into the eternal purposes You have for her and her family. Give her patience and a calm heart when family members disappoint; give her an added measure of wisdom when family members come to her with problems; give her added strength when family members require her assistance. Guide her prayers for her family, and give her joy in her family role.

67

Taking Time to Reflect

I remember the days of old;
I meditate on all Your doings;
I muse on the work of Your hands.
(Psalm 143:5 NAS)

What is it that we should "reflect" on? First, all of the many ways in which God has made Himself known to us in the past. Second, all of the many things God has done for His people, now and in the past, including one's own self. Third, all of the creative ways God works and accomplishes His purposes. A person who recognizes God's presence, God's blessings, and God's creative power, is a person who finds renewal!

Help Your child today to see the benefits of taking the time to pause, rest, and reflect. Bring to her heart and mind Your awesome nature, Your incredible blessings, and Your amazing creative power. Push out of her mind any thoughts that seek to compete with Your presence. Enfold her in Yourself.

68

Hiding More Scripture in One's Memory

Thy word have I hid in mine heart, that I might not sin against thee.
(Psalm 119:11 KJV)

The word "heart" in Hebrew thinking refers to the *will* of a person, not to emotions. To hide the word of God in one's heart, one must have made a decision, "I will remember and do what God commands and act on faith to pursue what God promises." In order to hide the word in one's heart, of course, means first knowing God's Word and purposefully recalling it whenever one faces a key decision or choice. To that end, memorization of Scripture is a great idea! The end goal is that we do not break our relationship with God by disobeying Him. Neither do we limit our rewards by not looking for them or working for them.

Convict Your beloved, O Lord, to HIDE Your Word in her heart—to know your Word, memorize Your Word, and choose to recall Your Word as she makes all choices and decisions. Give her a deep desire to do Your will at all times, in all situations, and in all relationships.

69

Safety in Travel

The LORD shall preserve your going out and your coming in
From this time forth, and even forevermore.
(Psalm 121:8 NKJV)

God does not send His people on journeys without helping them to arrive at His chosen destination and to do there His work. Jesus portrayed this in telling His disciples to take a boat to the other side of the Sea of Galilee. Even though a great storm nearly capsized their small fishing boat, they *arrived*! Jesus had full confidence they would—He had so much trust in His Heavenly Father that he fell asleep during the storm. Trust God to tell you *where* to go, and then trust Him to help you get there and do the work He has for you to do. The key, of course, is only embarking on journeys that He authorizes.

Give Your child sensitivity today, O Father, to walk only where You command her to walk. Give her deep trust that You are with her every step of the way, and that You will not only bring her to Your destination, but will help her to accomplish there all that You desire for her to say and do.

70

Staying Focused on What Is Good

Whatever is . . . of good repute, if there is any excellence and if anything worthy of praise, dwell on these things.
(Philippians 4:8 NAS)

The word "repute" links the concepts of "report" and "reputation." Things of good repute are things that create a person's reputation for doing what is godly. We are to focus our attention on what God calls good, not what the world calls good. God has His own definitions for excellence—excellence throughout the Scriptures is a concept rooted in obedience of heart and performance of DEED. Always of "good repute" are those things that prompt a person to praise God for His enabling and accomplishing power.

Thank You, O Lord, for showing Your child what is good in Your eyes. Help him to build a godly reputation before You and others. Show him Your path of excellence and help him to walk in it.

> *We should never pray in contradiction to the Bible, and we should never read the Bible without praying that we might apply what we read.*
>
> —Anonymous

71

A Desire for What Is Pure

Cleanse your hands, you sinners; and purify your hearts, you double-minded.
(James 4:8b NKJV)

Impurities clog the works and mar one's witness. This is true in both the natural and spiritual realms. We are to do works that promote purity—including the way we conduct our lives and the ways we engage in practical and personal hygiene and appearance-enhancement. We are also to purify our minds—refusing to entertain anything that might be considered a polluting or "dirty" thought, attitude, or opinion. All thoughts should bring honor to Jesus Christ, just as all behaviors and relationships. We purify our emotions by refusing to harbor fear, worry, or hatred, replacing these negative emotions by an act of our will, and adopting faith, trust, and love. We purify our SPIRITS by spending more time in the presence of the Lord, finding more and more reasons to thank Him and praise Him.

Impart a desire to Your beloved one today for ALL that is pure. Give her conviction about what needs to be "cleaned up" in her life—especially her physical and material life, her habits, and her thought life. Let every aspect of her life be a clean and polished surface capable of reflecting You to the world.

72

More Patience

Be patient, brethren, until the coming of the Lord. The farmer waits for the precious produce of the soil, being patient about it, until it

gets the early and late rains. You too be patient; strengthen your hearts, for the coming of the Lord is near.
(James 5:7–8 NAS)

Patience doesn't mean waiting for "never." It means waiting for the fullness of God's timing and the maximum benefit of God's blessing. Patience does not mean sitting down and waiting for the future to unfold. It means working diligently with faith that the future *will* arrive according to God's plans and purposes, and in perfect timing on His schedule.

Give Your child, O Lord, an added measure of patience today. Reveal to him a positive option to any and every moment that might produce anger or frustration. Show him how to make the most of the "extra time" required in waiting. Give him a calm mind and heart.

73

Developing a Reputation for Integrity

[The Lord said through the prophet Isaiah:]
"I know their works and their thoughts."
(Isaiah 66:18 NAS)

Integrity is an alignment of a person's thoughts (beliefs, values), words, and deeds—and especially as they are displayed over time. Our choice of habits builds our character, for good or for bad, and those who build GOOD character and display it consistently have integrity. The person with integrity can be counted on by others to say what he thinks and believes, and to act in a way that reflects his words and beliefs. He is "predictably" godly.

Help Your child, O Lord, to be consistent in what she believes, says, and does. Show her when things fall out of alignment. Give her the courage it takes to build godly character and to develop a reputation for doing what is right in Your eyes.

74

Developing a Reputation for Virtue

Since the day we heard of it, we have not ceased to pray for you and to ask that you may be filled with the knowledge of His will in all spiritual wisdom and understanding, so that you will walk in a manner worthy of the Lord, to please Him in all respects, bearing fruit in every good work, and increasing in the knowledge of God. (Colossians 1:9–10 NAS)

Virtue is a quality generally associated with being morally good or righteous—righteous refers to being in right standing with God, in other words, living in a way that GOD defines as right or good. Through the centuries the Church has described virtue in terms of justice, moderation, hope, charity, chastity (purity and fidelity). These are the character traits that remain above reproach. The purpose of virtue is to bear fruit—to be a living example of Christ's power dwelling within, in a way that attracts others to desire Christ in their lives.

O Lord, help Your child today to walk in a manner that is truly pleasing to You in ALL respects, bearing the most noble of fruit—a witness that increases the population of Heaven.

If you can't pray as you want to, pray as you can. God knows what you mean.

—Vance Havner

75

Living a Balanced Life

"Pray for us to the LORD . . . that the LORD your God may tell us the way in which we should walk and the thing that we should do." (Jeremiah 42:2–3 NAS)

God has a way for us to believe, to think, to speak, and to act. His desire is that these four areas of our life are in sync—functioning in harmony. Our interior life and exterior life are to have identical characteristics. The way we function alone, and the way we function in the presence and in relationship with others, is to be seamless. We are to live in balance. We cannot engineer this on our own, of course. We must trust God, our MAKER and the writer of the Owner's Manual for our lives, to reveal His plan to us and to give us the courage and ability to fulfill that plan. Our part is to go to Him for counsel, and then to do what He says. His part is to produce balance and integrity within us.

Help Your child today, O Lord, to trust You for greater balance in her life.

76

Pursuing What Is Honorable

Whatever is honorable . . . dwell on these things.
(Philippians 4:8 NAS)

Things that are honorable are those thing that we admire and respect; we find them worthy and desirable. Honorable things are nearly always manifested by honorable people; we sense a disconnect if dishonorable people do honorable things—something about their deed has a taint of shadow or self-serving pride. It is a good thing to spend time deciding not only how we want to live, but the character traits we want to develop. Such a list of "things to be" is far more important in the long run of life than any list of "things to do."

Give Your child a strong sense of what is honorable. Call him to display the best You have put in him, consistently and selflessly.

77

Freedom from Anxiety

Be anxious for nothing, but in everything by prayer and supplication with thanksgiving let your requests be made known to God. (Philippians 4:6 NAS)

Anxiety is garden-variety fear. It is synonymous with worry and fretting. Anxiety always includes elements of frustration and fear. And, it generally leads to discouragement, which can lead to depression, which can lead to despair. There is no benefit from ANXIETY! The antidote is to pray about what concerns us or causes us to feel frustration and fear. Ask God to deal with the situation or the person that you believe is causing your angst, and then move on with thanksgiving in your heart that God, who has always been faithful to you in the past, is continuing to extend His mercy and love to you. He is in control of all things!

Help Your child today, O Lord, to turn all frustrations, worries, anxiety, and fears over to You. Help her to pry her own hands off the worrisome situation to allow You to be fully in control!

78

Clarity about What Is True

I am Your servant; give me understanding,
That I may know Your testimonies.
(Psalm 119:125 NAS)

God will show us what is right and wrong—what is good and evil, what is true and false—if we will ask Him to reveal His truth to us. We can know what is truth, in part because we can know the full embodiment of TRUTH, the Lord Jesus Christ. All that Jesus said and did was good, right, and true. God never denies a request for greater understanding about Jesus!

Make Your truth very clear to Your servant today, O Lord! Reveal YOURSELF, I pray.

79

A Gentle Spirit

Let your gentle spirit be known to all men.
(Philippians 4:5 NAS)

Gentle in the Bible is not a synonym for either "wimp" or "doormat." To be gentle means to have a calm assurance that God is in charge of all things, and that every person is on HIS timetable and agenda for purification and wholeness. The person with a gentle spirit is strong and kind, using as little force as necessary to accomplish God's directives. Think of a giant, muscle-bound man tenderly holding a young child as he rescues it from danger—the child in one hand, the evil person seeking to harm the child being pinned down by the giant's foot in a way that restrains but does not crush. That is the Bible picture of gentleness.

Help Your servant to display gentleness at all time, O Lord. Show him the strength that is manifested in kindness.

80

Courage in the Face of Fear

[Moses said to the people of Israel:]
"Be strong and courageous, do not be afraid or tremble at them, for the LORD your God is the one who goes with you. He will not fail you or forsake you."
(Deuteronomy 31:6 NAS)

Our enemies DO scare us—their hatred is unfathomable, their behavior erratic, their goals are our destruction and death. The ONLY way to be strong and courageous in the face of enemies is to KNOW with absolute certainty that God not only goes with us, but that He fights our battles for us if we will trust Him to do so!

O Lord, give You servant today the confidence that only You can give. Walk with her, fight for her, and uphold her every step of today.

81

Having Awe of Holy God

Let all the inhabitants of the world stand in awe of Him.
(Psalm 33:8b NAS)

To be filled with awe means to have an overwhelming feeling of amazement and respect, and often a little fear at suddenly feeling so personally insignificant or powerless. This is surely how it must be, however, if one is aware of God's holy presence. Perhaps the most amazing aspect of awe is that God *allows* us to experience His presence, and invites us to come ever closer for greater and greater intimacy with Him!

Give Your child today, O heavenly Father, an awe-filled moment with You!

82

Good Mentors

[The apostle Paul wrote:]
The things you have learned and received and heard and seen in me, practice these things, and the God of peace will be with you.
(Philippians 4:9 NAS)

The apostle Paul was not making a statement out of pride—rather, he knew that what he had manifested to the Colossians was a tremendous dependence UPON, humility BEFORE, and the conveyance of wisdom that comes only from clinging tightly TO Christ Jesus. The best mentors in life embody these same traits and we are wise to seek them out eagerly and emulate them. Further, we can openly seek to be a mentor to others if we are willing to live as Paul lived.

Help Your beloved one today, O Lord, to be eagerly in search of wise mentors who can help teach us how to live the Christian life fully and productively, and then, to be willing to mentor others as You lead and authorize.

83

Being a Good Role Model for Others

[Moses commanded:]
"These words, which I am commanding you today, shall be on your heart. You shall teach them diligently to your sons and shall talk of them when you sit in your house and when you walk by the way and when you lie down and when you rise up."
(Deuteronomy 6:6–7 NAS)

The best teaching comes in the form of role-modeling—of living out the application of truth and wisdom before others. Teaching is not just telling information or facts. It is adding understanding to information, and wisdom to understanding. It is an all-day process, and especially if one is raising children to become godly adults. We can only teach what we have been taught, and what we know with confidence "in our heart" about God. Our primary role, therefore, as a teacher and role model, is to learn from Jesus and keep our eyes firmly fixed on the life He modeled for us.

Help Your beloved servant today, O Lord to learn from You and then teach everything he learns to others—in both word and deed.

> *Prayer requires that we stand in God's presence ... proclaiming to ourselves and to others that without God we can do nothing.*
>
> —Henri Nouwen

84

Shared Laughter with Children

Our mouth was filled with laughter
And our tongue with joyful shouting;
Then they said among the nations,
"The Lord has done great things for them."
The Lord has done great things for us;
We are glad.
(Psalm 126:2–3 NAS)

Children laugh only when they feel free to laugh. That freedom comes when a child feels safe, loved, and has opportunities to express his exuberance and joy in an environment that is welcoming. A child laughs when he sees positive results from his own actions and creativity. He laughs when the foibles and fumbles of life go unpunished. He laughs when he is healthy, strong, and has his basic needs met. What is true for a child is also true for us! We adults must never laugh AT others, but rather, be quick to laugh WITH others. We are wise to create environments that allow for the joy of the Lord to be expressed with an abundance of laughter!

Fill Your child's life today with laughter, O Lord. Give her abundant opportunities to express gladness at the sheer wonders of life!

85

A Quickness in Showing Affection

[Jesus told a parable in which He said:]
"While he [the rebellious son] was still a long way off, his father saw him and felt compassion for him, and ran and embraced him and kissed him."
(Luke 15:20 NAS)

The father's embrace of his son was not only a great sign of personal affection and acceptance. It also was a preemptive move; this rebellious son *could* have been killed, according to the religious customs of that time, for his blatant disrespect—even disregard—of the father in demanding his inheritance and then departing from the community. The father was sparing the son's life, and openly offering him "newness" of life. What a wonderful thought that the Father is looking for us to turn to Him, and that He receives us with open arms, sparing us from evil and restoring us to the fullness of all He has planned for us!

Show Your child today, O Father, how much You love him and want Him to receive and pursue all that You have planned for His good.

86

The Ability to Give and Receive Love

[Jesus taught:]
"Give, and it will be given to you. They will pour into your lap a good measure—pressed down, shaken together, and running over."
(Luke 6:38 NAS)

We are to be both givers and receivers with others in the Body of Christ. For some, giving is easier than receiving—for others, receiving is easier than giving! We are wise to ask God to give us a balance. We *need* what others can give to us—especially their ideas, creativity, wisdom, faith, time, prayers, support . . . the list is long when it comes to what others have of value. We also *need* to give. It is an outflow that allows God to continue His inflow of love, mercy, and creativity. The ongoing process of giving and receiving is one that Jesus said causes increase, growth, and refinement—not only in us, but in others and in the Body of Christ as a whole.

Dear Lord, show Your servant new ways to give and receive.

87

Having Worthy Role Models

[The apostle Paul wrote:]
Let a man regard us in this manner, as servants of Christ and stewards of the mysteries of God.
(1 Corinthians 4:1 NAS)

We live in a world that seems obsessed with "celebrities." The power of celebrity is strong—it is a major influencer in our culture in every area of life. The apostle Paul wrote that we are to allow ourselves to admire and be influenced only by those who exalt Christ and who are His servants. We are to evaluate others on the basis of their Christ-like character and commitment to doing Christ's work in the world. Let those be the people we lift up!

Help Your child today, O Lord, to look beyond a person's fame, appearance, or cultural influence and to focus only on those traits that are godly. Do not let her be led astray into following or emulating any person who is not a believer in Christ Jesus.

88

A Willingness to Ask for What You Need

You do not have because you do not ask.
(James 4:2b NKJV)

God knows what we need even before we ask. Why ask? Because in our asking, we give evidence to our own selves that we have need and are relying upon God to meet that need. Sometimes people do not recognize the true nature of their own need until they give voice to it. At other times, we confuse our needs and wants, and it is only in voicing our requests that we are able to distinguish between need and want. Defining our need gives us an opportunity to evaluate our need against those things that God calls a true "need." The second thing that happens when we ask is that we "activate" our faith—indeed, asking is a direct act of faith, giving evidence of our trust in God to meet our need. God does not respond automatically to need. He always responds to faith, and to those who are turning to Him for His answers.

Prompt in Your child, O Lord, an accurate awareness of her true, deepest, and most pressing needs. Give her a willingness to bring those needs to You, trusting You to both hear and provide *all* that is needed to fulfill the tasks that You have set before her.

89

A Death that Is Truly Holy, Good, and Peaceful

May the God of peace Himself sanctify you entirely, and may your spirit and soul and body be preserved complete, without blame at the coming of our Lord Jesus Christ.
(1 Thessalonians 5:23 NAS)

True evil is always aimed at destroying our relationship with the Lord, and thus, denying us either a heavenly home or heavenly rewards. The role of our adversary is to "accuse" us—to make us doubt and question God's ability to sanctify and preserve us without any blame. The truth is: the bond of our relationship with God cannot be broken by the enemy once we have fully received Jesus as our Savior. This does not mean that we will not be the target or victim of evil on this earth—even evil that maims, or kills. It does mean that these attacks cannot keep us from God's eternal presence. Knowing that we are just one moment away from eternal life in heaven—a life that is whole and vibrant and filled with peace—can make all the difference as one faces death.

Father, I pray today that You will give Your beloved child the assurance that evil cannot strip away her salvation or destroy her relationship with You.

90

Refusing to Complain

[The apostle Paul wrote:]
"I have learned to be content in whatever circumstances I am. I know how to get along with humble means, and I also know how to live in prosperity; in any and every circumstance I have learned the secret of being filled and going hungry, both of having abundance and suffering need."
(Philippians 4:11–12 NAS)

The "state of our being" is not necessarily the "state of our current circumstances!" The ability to be content—satisfied and without whining complaint—is a spiritual trait and a mark of spiritual maturity. We can be content *within*, even as we seek to change outer circumstances to our advantage or to the advantage of the Gospel. It is a wonderful thing to be willing to live simply, to be able to move freely and comfortably in all levels of society, and to maintain a steady faith walk regardless of the situation in which one may find oneself.

Help Your child today, dear heavenly Father, to be content WITHIN herself, and thus, within her present circumstances. Help her to *work* for what You are leading her to do, rather than to *whine* about what she may be experiencing.

> *Our prayer and God's mercy are like two*
> *buckets in a well; while the one ascends,*
> *the other descends.*
>
> —Mark Hopkins

91

Welcoming Accountability

Search me, O God, and know my heart;
Try me and know my anxious thoughts;
And see if there be any hurtful way in me,
And lead me in the everlasting way.
(Psalm 139:23–24 NAS)

Accountability is a testing and searching process—an "auditing" of sorts, looking for discrepancies, errors, and a disparity between what a person desires to do and what a person actually does. At the heart of accountability is the concept of integrity, which is total alignment of what a person *thinks*, *says*, and *does*. God wants His people to be genuine, through and through. He wants His people to be consistent across time and circumstances, and in all relationships—always with unwavering trust in Him.

Lead Your child, O Lord, to self-examination so she might confess and be forgiven for all things displeasing to you. Show her, by the power of Your Holy Spirit, how to amend her ways to walk in righteousness. Give her the courage to confront her own fears and worries, and to recognize that You desire for her to trust You in these areas of her life. Prepare her for heaven a little more every day!

92
Faithful Prayer Partners

[Jesus taught:]
"If two of you agree on earth about anything that they may ask, it shall be done for them by My Father who is in heaven. For where two or three have gathered together in My name, I am there in their midst."
(Matthew 18:19–20 NAS)

The Jewish concept from ancient times has been that the truth is established out of the mouths of two or more witnesses. The truth of God's love is best expressed by "two or more." Jesus also held this as the standard for witnessing about Him, as He sent out His disciples two by two to spread the news of His ministry on earth. This basic organizational pattern helps maintain balance in the church—no one person is either responsible for or can claim credit for the work of Christ Jesus when it comes to healing, saving, and delivering those who suffer.

Give Your child, I pray, a faithful person with whom to study the Scriptures, pray, and witness to unbelievers. Assure her that YOU are in their midst as she joins with a fellow believer to pray for YOUR ministry to be fulfilled on this earth.

93

A New Song of Praise

Sing to Him a new song.
(Psalm 33:3 NKJV)

God desires a sacrifice of praise—not because God needs affirmation, but because praise is always an expression that reminds *us* of God's lasting, enduring, never-changing nature. God is infinitely good, infinitely loving, merciful, creative, powerful, and wise—now and forever. He alone is worthy of our highest praise!

Put a new melody into the heart of Your child today. Let her burst forth in singing to You what is in her heart. Give her fluidity of lyrics, truly bringing up the feelings of her deepest core in a free and freeing expression to You. Let her hear Your applause, I pray, for her praise offering.

94

A Quickness to Rejoice with Those Who Are Rejoicing

Rejoice with those who rejoice.
(Romans 12:15 NAS)

Those who are quick to rejoice with others are those who are free of envy or jealousy. True generosity of heart is evidenced by those who applaud the good performances of others, delight in their rewards, voice appreciation for their acts of kindness, and give honor to their good works. Be quick to appreciate the good in others, and to delight in the good things that come their way! Who knows? They just may share their good blessings with you!

Give Your child a willingness—yes, even an *eagerness*—to rejoice with those who have had good things come their way. Free her from all jealousy and envy.

95

Good News!

Like cold water to a weary soul,
So is good news from a distant land.
(Proverbs 25:25 NAS)

Everybody likes good news! It refreshes the emotions, the mind, and the spirit of a person. It renews strength and yields courage. It inspires renewed hope, faith, and acts of love. Every Christian is called to be a Gospel-speaker, knowing that the word Gospel literally means the "Good News" of Christ Jesus. We each face a decision when it comes to whether we will focus on the good things in life, or on the bad. We have a decision to make about whether we will speak about the good, or the bad. We must choose to be a positive influencer, not a purveyor of what is negative. Making choices for the positive puts us into the company of all who are ENCOURAGERS—those who uplift, edify, and breathe new life into the souls of others.

Help Your child, O Lord, to be a speaker of good news to others. Give her an ear to hear the good news coming her way. O Lord, *send* a new message of good news to her about Your love and care!

96

Conception

[The Lord said through Isaiah the prophet:]
"Behold, I will do something new,
Now it will spring forth;
Will you not be aware of it?"
(Isaiah 43:19a NAS)

Conception is always a prerequisite for a birthing! That is true for babies. It is also true for ideas. The good news is that our Creator is always leading us as His children to His "next new thing." The conception begins deep within us. We are incubators—wonderful and personal—for all of God's unfolding creative plans and purposes.

Help your beloved one to exercise his creativity today—to do something or learn something that brings about a greater testimony and a great understanding of You. Give him the ability to conceive the "new thing"" that You desire to do on the earth!

97

Freedom

For the law of the Spirit of life in Christ Jesus has set you free from the law of sin and of death.
(Romans 8:2 NAS)

We are ruled by "law." Law is a matter of parameters, boundaries, constraints. Before we came to a saving knowledge of Christ Jesus, we were ruled by sin—our sinful nature dictated our responses to life, the consequence of those responses was always something that stole, destroyed, or killed a part of us. The new "law of the Spirit of life in Christ Jesus" puts us into a very different realm—our "new nature" as a new creation in Christ also dictates our responses to life, but in a way that promotes eternal values, earthly blessings, right thinking and believing, and godly living. Only a believer in Christ Jesus can know TRUE freedom, from the inside out.

Impart, O Lord, a new awareness of the freedom that You have given to Your beloved servant. Let him be ruled by impulses of the Spirit that generate godliness and life in all its wonderful forms!

98

Full Assurance that Your Name is in the Lamb's Book of Life

[John had a revelation of Heaven:]
Nothing unclean, and no one who practices abomination and lying, shall ever come into it, but only those whose names are written in the Lamb's book of life.
(Revelation 21:27 NAS)

Having an *assurance* that you are Heaven-bound is a matter of faith. We must accept that what Jesus said He would do, He has done and will always do—He is the One who makes us whole, including a wholeness of relationship with God the Father. We must believe that no matter what we do, if our hearts have been infused and filled with God's Holy Spirit, our *desire* and motivation will be to do what is godly. We will not *want* to engage in anything that is contrary to God's highest and best for us. If we find ourselves sinning, the cure is simple: Ask for more of the Holy Spirit, and then rely on Him with even greater dependence to take you from where you are to where He has planned for you to be—with Him for all eternity!

Grant a deep assurance to Your child today, O Lord, that she will live with You forever in Heaven, and that every moment between now and the day she dies, You are with her, dwelling within her and moving through her to bless others.

99

Steadfastness in Following Christ

Let us hold fast the confession of our hope without wavering, for He who promised is faithful.
(Hebrews 10:23 NAS)

The psalmist asked God to "renew a steadfast spirit" within him. (Psalm 51:10 NKJV) To be steadfast is to have a firm and constant resolve—the steadfast person is not easily swayed or pushed off course. Steadfastness is ultimately a spiritual quality. It refers to an unwavering faith, hope, and love—rooted in the absolute faithfulness of God's love, mercy, and grace. We can only be steadfast if we are one hundred percent convinced of God's steadfastness towards us, which enables us to believe God's promises and believe that our sins are forgiven and our home is in Heaven. If you find yourself "wavering" in what you believe, check your beliefs regarding the faithfulness of God. The TRUTH is that

God is faithful to us, His children—at all times, in all situations, now and forever.

Precious Lord, help Your child to be unwavering in her commitment to You. Renew a steadfast spirit in her. Help her to walk in Your ways to bring glory to Your name—always.

100

Being an Example of God's Goodness on Display

So you may walk in the way of goodness,
And keep to the paths of righteousness.
(Proverbs 2:20 NKJV)

Goodness and godliness are virtually synonymous in the Scriptures. The GOOD news is that we can know the "godly" way to walk out life's journey—it is found in the Bible's commands coupled with the Holy Spirit's daily directives. Read the Word. Ask the Holy Spirit to lead you. As you obey, your life becomes a walking billboard for God's goodness!

Help Your beloved one today, Heavenly Father, to reflect YOU to the world—to be a "case study" of your goodness and mercy.

God not only gives us answers to our prayers, but with every answer gives us something of Himself.

—Unknown

101

Feeling Worthy

We exhorted, and comforted, and charged every one of you, as a father does his own children, that you would walk worthy of God who calls you into His own kingdom and glory.
(1 Thessalonians 2:11 NKJV)

Many people struggle with feeling "worthy" to receive the best blessings of life—the reason for their feelings of inadequacy are often rooted in *mankind's* definition of worthiness, not *God's* definition. God says we ARE worthy of the shed blood of Jesus Christ, and when we accept Jesus as our Savior, we ARE worthy of all the riches of Heaven as a joint heir of Christ. God counts us worthy to appropriate and use the Name of Jesus. Our challenge is to obey God's commands and WALK out our life in a way that pleases God, which is simultaneously a way that prepares us for our life in Heaven one day. The apostle Paul noted to the Thessalonians that this was his exhortation and charge, but also his word of comfort. We must do this, we can do it, and God delights in our doing it!

Help Your beloved one today, O Lord, to walk out this day in a way that is worthy of Your greatest blessings and approval.

102

Living in a Way that Does Not Offend

We give no offense in anything, that our ministry may not be blamed.
(2 Corinthians 6:3 NKJV)

We can never ensure completely that we won't offend others—in truth, unbelievers are always slightly offended by Christ in us until they receive Him for themselves. We can, however, do our utmost to avoid being *purposefully offensive* to others. Most of us know what pushes the hot buttons of those close to us. Most of us know what is culturally impolite or offensive. If we can avoid causing offense, we have a much better chance of having our message about God's plan of salvation heard and accepted by others.

O Lord, help Your beloved one today to walk in a way that is considered pleasing. Keep her from even "casually" causing offense by things she does or leaves undone.

103

Feeling Beloved by God

[God sent the angel Gabriel to tell Daniel:]
"You are greatly beloved."
(Daniel 9:23 NKJV)

Perhaps no greater message can ever be heard by a person than this: "God loves you." God speaks this message continually, but because of our own disbelief or interfering lies from others that function as "static on the line," we often do not "receive" the message. Consider Daniel's position—he had been forcibly removed from his homeland and had been living as a resident alien in Babylon for decades. Although he had enjoyed great favor from various emperors, he had also received a terrifying vision of a ram and a goat that left him physically sick, and he had gone to God in prayer about this vision. It was as Daniel was confessing his sin, and the sin of his people, that the angel came to speak to him. One Bible version says the angel Gabriel said, "You are highly esteemed." Daniel was beloved by God, counted as worthy of receiving the vision and its interpretation. God's love for US is what give us all the self-esteem we need! God considers us worthy of receiving forgiveness of sin and life everlasting through acceptance of the sacrificial death of His Son, Jesus, as being on our behalf. God further shows His love to us by giving us the ability to read, understand, and apply the truth of His Word. As in all things pertaining to the spiritual realm, we must CHOOSE to believe that we are loved by God. It is an act of our faith to declare, "I am God's beloved."

Today, O Lord, assure Your child once again that he is loved by you and is highly esteemed as your chosen servant in his world, at this time, in the very circumstances that lie ahead for him. Give him the confidence that he is counted as worthy by You to bear Your family name and character!

104

Feeling Loved by Others

I am my beloved's,
And his desire is toward me.
(Song of Solomon 7:10 NKJV)

Every person needs to feel the love of other people who are representatives of God's love "with skin on." Physical and emotional affection are encouraging, comforting, and vital to health. Ask God to send you faithful friends and family members who will openly show love to you—in attitude, words, and deeds. Even as you receive love from others, freely return it in ways that are morally right before God. All acts of hatred on this planet are the result of a lack of sufficient love!

Send someone today, O Lord, to show love to Your child. Let that person wrap his or her arms around Your child as an expression of Your everlasting arms holding Your child in a warm embrace.

105

Choosing to Love Even When You Don't Feel Like It

Put on love, which is the bond of perfection.
(Colossians 3:14 NKJV)

Love is a choice we make. It is an act of our will. It is something that produces greater wholeness in us, as well as to the person receiving our love. In all ways, love is an act of *giving*—with physical, emotional, verbal, and spiritual dimensions. At times, we encounter those who seem decidedly "unlovable"—in those cases, we must ask the Lord to help us see that person as *He* sees him, and to give what He desires for him to receive. Even when we don't "feel" love, we must extend love.

Help Your servant to show love to others in ways that are genuine and meaningful. Give him many opportunities *this very day* to be an extension of Your love.

106

A Glimpse of Heaven and God's Glory

[Stephen said:]
"Look! I see the heavens opened and the Son of Man standing at the right hand of God!"
(Acts 7:56 NKJV)

Is there anything that you find fearful about Heaven? Ask God to edit your perception and to give you a glimpse into what a "perfect" life will be like. Consider what is flawed, imperfect, hurtful, or uncomfortable in your life today. Heaven will have none of that! The best part of Heaven is not seeing your deceased relatives and friends. It is not walking on streets of gold. The best part of Heaven is JESUS and the opportunity to live in His near presence forever, joining with others in praise at the foot of God's eternal throne! Nothing on earth is worth missing any part of Heaven's reward.

Heavenly Father, renew an excitement about Heaven in the life of Your beloved servant. Let him know with renewed assurance that his heavenly home will make all struggle for the Gospel on this earth worthwhile.

107

A Desire to Obey God's Commands

Whoever keeps His word, truly the love of God is perfected in him. By this we know that we are in Him. He who says He abides in Him ought himself also to walk just as He walked.
(1 John 2:5–6 NKJV)

The main way we show our love for God is by obeying His commandments, which include a commandment to love others as we love ourselves. It is not "love" to harbor hatred, bitterness, or resentment against others. It also is not "love" to have low self-esteem or low self-worth! We must obey God in all things, including His commands to forgive ourselves and others, and to "bless" ourselves and others with the assurance that we have a bright and glorious future, now and forever. Only when we obey God can His love fill us to overflowing. Only as we obey can we be His representatives of mercy and kindness.

Kindle a renewed desire to know and obey ALL of Your commands, O Lord. Help Your beloved servant to see that obedience is the key to experiencing the fullness of Your love.

108

Knowing God's Will with Certainty

"... that you may stand perfect and complete in the will of God." (Colossians 4:12 NKJV)

To be "complete" in this verse also means to be "fully assured." God desires that we be fully confident of two great truths: He is at work in us, making us more and more whole (perfect), and, He desires that we be strong in our belief that the will of God is the very *best* way to live, now and always.

Assure Your child today, O Lord, that he is smack dab in the middle of Your plan and purpose for him. And if he isn't, guide him to that point and let him know You are perfecting him.

109

Walking Daily in the Spirit

Walk in the Spirit, and ye shall not fulfil the lust of the flesh. (Galatians 5:16 KJV)

It is our decision to make! We must each decide to walk in the Spirit—which means asking the Spirit daily to guide us and counsel us. Then, as He leads, we must be quick to follow. The Holy Spirit does not lead God's beloved children into sin, or allow God's beloved ones to be overwhelmed by temptation. The places to which the Spirit leads, and the people with whom the Spirit connects us, are for God's purposes and our eternal reward. The Spirit does not lead us into situations that provide only momentary fulfillment of earthly passions.

Help Your child today, O Lord, to *choose* to rely on the Spirit for constant guidance throughout the day.

110

Running Life's Race to Victorious Completion

[The apostle Paul wrote:]
I press on toward the goal for the prize of the upward call of God in Christ Jesus.
[Philippians 3:14 NAS)

Life is a multi-day marathon, not a sprint. Each day has its own leg of the race to run. We must pursue God's purposes for us with daily diligence and effort, *pressing* ourselves forward to do all that we can to extend the Gospel and influence others for eternity. That is the *only* way to find ourselves at death's door with no regrets.

Give Your servant a heart that desires You more than anything or any one. Give her a *press-forward* attitude and strength to run today's race.

111

Withstanding Temptation

[Jesus said,]
"Watch and pray, lest you enter into temptation."
(Matthew 26:41a NKJV)

What are we to "watch for?" We are to be keenly aware of the enemy's work in the world, and more specifically, his attempts to influence our personal lives and relationships. This is not to say that we must adopt a preoccupation with the devil. The exact opposite! We are to preoccupy ourselves with the truth of God and to voice His truth in PRAYER. It is only when we have a heads-up attitude toward the lies of the enemy, however, that we are able to resist him and refrain from swallowing his deceit or entering into his temptations. Jesus gave this command to His disciples in the Garden of Gethsemane, just hours before His crucifixion. He knew that the enemy would do his utmost in those hours to deceive the disciples into believing that Jesus was *not* the Son of God and that their following Him had been an exercise in futility, with no reward and no future. They easily could have been tempted to abandon Christ completely. We, too, whether we realize it or not, are fed similar lies daily. The devil often whispers to our soul, "Being a Christian is an unfavorable, demeaning, unrewarding way to live." Be on the alert for those lies! Pray that God will silence people who speak such the lies, and refuse to buy into their message.

Help Your child today, O Heavenly Father, to be on high alert against the devil's tactics, and to stay in prayer—voicing petitions based upon Your truth—to bolster courage and strength against all lies and deceit. Keep Your child from yielding to temptation today, I pray.

112

Maintaining Self-Control

The fruit of the Spirit is . . . self-control.
(Galatians 5:22–23 NKJV)

The phase "self-control" has also been translated "temperance" or "moderation in all things that are good." It takes an act of will to say "no" to evil, but also to an unnecessary second helping. Is it a sin to over-indulge on life's pleasures? It is if that indulgence keeps a person from being all he or she can be, if that indulgence functions as a stumbling block for others, or if that indulgence keeps a person from generously sharing his blessings with others. God's Spirit moves within us to help us make the right choices, in quality and quantity, and to make right decisions about how much we give and how much we keep for our own use.

Help Your child today, O Lord, to make choices and decisions in complete compliance with the Spirit's directives.

When you pray, believe that you will receive.

—Oral Roberts

113

Encouragement

David encouraged himself in the LORD his God.
(1 Samuel 30:6 KJV)

What did David do to "encourage" himself? To encourage literally means to "impart courage." David knew that he bore the responsibility for encouraging or motivating himself when he was down. David was facing a situation in 1 Samuel 30 in which he and his army had returned home to find all of their wives, children, animals, and belongings taken captive by an enemy. The soldiers were so distraught that they began to talk about killing David! In encouraging himself, David likely did these three things: One, he turned to the Lord, shutting out the ideas and words of man. Two, he likely sang to his own heart the words of songs he may have written—very possibly songs of praise about the sovereign nature of God and God's desire to bless His people. Three, he renewed his commitment to trust God in all things. After he had done this, he asked the Lord, "What shall I do?" He asked that question in faith and strength, not in the quagmire of devastating emotional turmoil or fear.

Help Your beloved one today, O Lord, to encourage himself in YOU. Help Him to turn all of His focus on Your ability and love, and Your desire to restore and reconcile.

114

Opportunities to Extend Encouragement to Others

Let us consider how to stimulate one another to love and good deeds ... encouraging one another; and all the more as you see the day drawing near.
(Hebrews 10:24–25 NAS)

We all love to be encouraged. The encouragement we receive must be extended to others. The best encouragement is the encouragement to pursue our walk with the Lord and to pursue *His* potential for us—which is always marked by a generous outpouring of good words and good gifts/deeds. Encouragement is VITAL for surviving tough times—whether those difficult experiences are individual-caused, rooted in family or society errors, or are natural catastrophes. The Bible tells us that the activity of the enemy will escalate as the day draws closer to the Lord's return. Encouragement of other believers is especially important so that we might withstand the devil's temptations and be fully ready to greet the Lord upon His arrival—both at His Second Coming and at His next appearing in our personal lives!

Heavenly Father, help Your servant to be a source of vibrant and enthusiastic encouragement—to believe in You, trust You, and obey You. Help him to stimulate others to generous giving and noble works.

> *Human life is a constant want, and*
> *ought to be a constant prayer.*
>
> —Samuel Osgood.

115

Knowing the Right Thing to Do—and Doing It

These joined with their brethren, their nobles, and entered into a curse and an oath to walk in God's Law, which was given by Moses the servant of God, and to observe and do all the commandments of the LORD our Lord, and His ordinances and His statutes.
(Nehemiah 10:29 NKJV)

It is one thing to "observe"—just to watch and know, or even to commemorate and celebrate—what God commands. It is another thing to fulfill, or actually "do," what God commands. As an example, virtually everybody—no matter their race, nationality, or culture—believes that love and mercy are right things to express. People routinely applaud and reward those who show love and mercy—but not everybody loves or extends mercy! Be a doer, and not just a "knower" or observer.

Help Your beloved one today, O Lord, both to know and do Your will for her on this earth. Give her the courage to speak up, stand up, and act as You lead her to do so.

116

Receiving Justice in One's Favor

[Jesus taught:]
"Shall God not avenge His own elect who cry out day and night to Him, though He bears long with them? I tell you that He will avenge them speedily. Nevertheless, when the Son of Man comes, will He really find faith on the earth?"
(Luke 18:6–8 NKJV)

Jesus gave the conclusion above to a story about a widow who returned again and again to a judge as she sought justice for a wrong committed against her. The judge, even though he claimed to have no regard for man or fear of God, finally granted her petition because she was so insistent and persistent. Jesus likened her to those who cry out to God insistently and persistently until they receive justice in their favor. Why does God require us to come again and again with our petitions? One of the reasons may be so that *we* will be aware of our own great need for God and also be more keenly aware of our true desires. God does not respond to our "whim and wish du jour"—indeed, there is nothing in the Bible that says God responds to all need. Rather, God responds consistently to our persistent expressions of *faith* that He can and will provide justice for us, and our expressions of commitment that we are going to persist in faith until He does so.

O Lord, help Your beloved child today to cling to You in prayer and faith until she receives Your answers. In Your answers are justice and mercy. Help her to receive both, according to Your purposes.

117

Speaking Truth with Love

[The apostle Paul desired for the believers:]
"that we should no longer be children, tossed to and fro and carried about with every wind of doctrine ... but, speaking the truth in love, may grow up in all things into Him who is the head—Christ—from whom the whole body, joined and knit together by what every joint supplies, according to the effective working by which every part does its share, causes growth of the body for the edifying of itself in love."
(Ephesians 4:14–16 NKJV)

A flow of love among believers allows for admonishment—godly wisdom given in the face of error—because a loving Church *wants* to be healthy, and to grow both spiritually and in relationships. Love is the attitude that should wrap every form of communication between believers. The person who hears truth expressed with an attitude of love is far more likely to receive the truth, and to heed it.

Help Your child, O Lord, to speak with love today. Do not let her back away from sharing Your truth, or refrain from speaking up for what is right according to Your Word. Help her find a way to boldly express the truth of Christ Jesus without any rancor, hate, bitterness, or desire for personal aggrandizement.

118

Overcoming Anger

The works of the flesh are . . . outbursts of wrath.
(Galatians 5:19–20 NKJV)

A person may seem to have been born with a "quick temper," but it is not God's desire that this temper erupt in a way that causes harm to others. Anger is a God-given emotion intended to motivate us to right a wrong, or to remedy an injustice. We must use our anger to inspire us toward greater good, not a display of ill will, retaliation, or vengeance. As with all emotions, we are to control anger with our will and ask the Holy Spirit to direct our anger toward the implementation of *His* purposes. Our emotions are not to rule us—we are to rule them.

Give Your assistance, gracious and holy Father, to Your servant that he might use the anger he feels to motivate him toward doing good.

> *Prayer crowns God with the honor and glory due to His name, and God crowns prayer with assurance and comfort.*
>
> —Thomas Brooks

119

Accepting Godly Admonition

Let the word of Christ richly dwell within you, with all wisdom teaching and admonishing one another with psalms and hymns and spiritual songs, singing with thankfulness in your hearts to God. (Colossians 3:16 NAS)

Admonition tends to have a twinge of negativity associated with it. In most cases, an admonition is a mild but earnest rebuke—it presents strong advice either for or against doing something. In the church, admonition is to be accompanied by psalms and hymns and spiritual songs that are filled with thanksgiving! Certainly, that setting for admonition can make admonition easier to take. The greater truth, however, is that when admonition is properly delivered, it is for our *good*—now and in eternity! Admonition is both preventive and corrective—it should be offered and received with an understanding that the ultimate goal of admonition is that a person be in precisely the right position for God's outpouring of blessing! True godly admonition is a little like saying, "If you just move over two steps to the right, you will be right under the open window of Heaven so you can receive the fullness of the goodness God is about to pour out." Admonition should never be rooted in a person's personal desire to manipulate or control. Neither should it be used to get people to line up with man-made cultural norms. Admonition is best used when eternal reward is on the verge of being missed! If you are being admonished by someone, accept their admonition if it is tied to God's rewards now and forever.

Help Your child, O Lord, to receive godly admonition, and on the flip side, to refrain from giving admonition that isn't godly. Help her to be thankful that others care enough to warn her or encourage her toward Your greatest blessings and rewards.

Every prayer should end, "Thy will be done."

—J. L. Dargatz

120

Recognizing and Turning Away from Idolatry

[God spoke through Moses:]
"You shall not make for yourself an idol, or any likeness of what is in heaven above or on the earth beneath or in the water under the earth. You shall not worship them or serve them; for I, the LORD your God, am a jealous God."
(Exodus 20:4–5 NAS)

The apostle Paul identified idolatry as a "deed of the flesh." (Galatians 5:20) It is not necessarily an object. It may be a habit or a persistent attitude. An idol is anything that a person "serves," and relies upon for favor in return—"favor" includes social status, material prosperity, or any other form of blessing. God's word to His people is that *He* alone is our source of all blessing. *He* alone is worthy to be praised and to be served. It is sometimes difficult to identify the idols in our own lives. We must ask God to help us see anything that we are trusting apart from Him.

Lord, help Your servant today to trust and serve You alone as the source of his life. Help him to recognize all idols in his life and to destroy them. Help him to refrain from regarding *anything* and *any person* as being in Your place as provider, protector, or source of supply.

121

Confessing and Repenting of Sin

If you confess with your mouth the Lord Jesus and believe in your heart that God has raised him from the dead, you will be saved. For with the heart one believes unto righteousness, and with the mouth confession is made unto salvation.
(Romans 10:9–10 NKJV)

To confess is to "admit"—to own up to one's sins rather than try to run from them, deny them, or attempt to justify the. Confession is a verbal statement, not an unvoiced "idea." This outward statement acts on prior belief that Jesus is the Christ. It is the admission, not just one's belief, that puts a person into position to receive the full gift of spiritual transformation offered by God.

O Lord, let Your beloved child be quick today to confess her sins, to seek Your forgiveness, and to gain the help of the Holy Spirit for true repentance and an ongoing walk in righteousness.

122

Freedom from Strife

Do all things without murmurings and disputings.
(Philippians 2:14 KJV)

Strife comes in two varieties: one is an inner attempt to get or achieve something through intense work; the second can be a bitter, even violent, conflict with others to win something. In both cases, a person is seeking to gain something out of personal ambition—the victory usually requires the defeat of others, and it nearly always involves bitter, angry, hateful words. In the church, strife can tear believers apart, often as the result of intense debate, rumors, and hurtful gossip. The good news of the Gospel is that we do not need to strive to gain *anything*. The Holy Spirit both empowers us to excel, and also sets in motion all circumstances around us for God's desired victories to be ours.

Give You beloved one the ability to trust You fully for the victories and rewards You have for her. Let her gain the understanding that she does not need to talk her way into success; nor does she need to strive through good works to gain either Your attention or Your favor.

123

Deliverance from Evil

[Jesus taught His disciples to pray:]
"Deliver us from evil."
(Matthew 6:13 NAS)

Only God can truly DELIVER us from the evil one. We can resist the devil by our proclamations of faith, but we cannot defeat him without God's help. Rather than address any comments TO the devil, we are wise to pray, "O God, deliver us from evil. YOU, O Lord, defeat the devil in my life. Remind the enemy of my soul about his eternal fate!" The more we bring up the name of Jesus, the more the enemy retreats.

Father, I pray today for YOU to deliver Your beloved one from evil. Drive the devil far from him, and bring him to wholeness.

124

Deliverance from Disputes, Dissensions, and Factions

The works of the flesh are evident, which are . . . contentions . . . selfish ambitions . . . dissensions.
(Galatians 5:19-20 NKJV)

God's desire is always that His people live in peaceful harmony with one another. When the body of Christ is ill-at-ease, it often becomes sick! (Disease is often the result of dis-ease.) There is tremendous value in seeking to work with people, rather than against people, and to seek to join forces rather than scatter resources. Few arguments are worth their bitter end, few contentions are worth the struggle unless they are admonitions that establish the truth of

Christ Jesus. His foremost truth, of course, is His identity as Prince of Peace!

Give Your servant, O Lord, a desire to get along with others to the very best of his ability, at all times and in all situations. Let him accommodate diversity for the sake of unity, and for the sake of witness to Your truth.

125

Deliverance from Immorality, Impurity, and Sensuality

The works of the flesh are . . . adultery, fornication, uncleanness, lewdness.
(Galatians 5:19 NKJV)

Sexual relationships link people together in ways that are never really "casual," rarely "completely consensual," and never "without spiritual impact." They cause injury to the self as well as to others. God's desire is for His people to live in purity and according to an order that strengthens a person spiritually, physically, mentally, and emotionally—and in turn, strengthens the family. We need to be clear on definitions: adultery is sex between two people, one of whom is married; fornication is sex between two unmarried people, lewdness is a preoccupation about sex (including pornography), and uncleanness is anything that violates God's laws about sexual purity, including various forms of sexual perversion and sexual abuse. God says "no" to sexual sins . . . and His prohibition is for *our* sake.

Help Your servant, O Lord, to refrain from anything that You prohibit regarding sexual behavior. Forgive what has been done in the past; give resolve and strength to act in purity going forward. Help Your servant to refrain from association with those who are intent on seduction and sexual sin.

126

Sobriety

The works of the flesh are . . . drunkenness, revelries, and the like.
(Galatians 5:19–20 NKJV)

Many people draw a conclusion that God is against people having fun, or enjoying a "good time." That is not at all the case! What God does oppose is people indulging their own physical lusts for substances and stimulation in a way that excludes giving honor to God—including going to excess in partying to the point that they lose control of their God-given common sense. The word "revelries" refers to celebrations that include *excessive* drinking, eating, dancing (in the ancient world, usually lewd dancing), and noise. We think of these as "Roman orgies" today. In our own culture, countless people are killed, maimed, assaulted, raped, and emotionally scarred—either intentionally or accidentally—every day as a result of too much alcohol consumption. Nobody has ever been injured by sobriety.

Help Your servant, Lord God, to say "no" to all things that are a substitute for Your joy, and to all things that can result in harm to self or others through excess. Give Your servant strong resolve to live in sobriety.

127

Walking in the Light

If we walk in the light as He is in the light, we have fellowship with one another, and the blood of Jesus Christ His Son cleanses us from all sin.
(1 John 1:7 NKJV)

Those who truly are being guided by the Holy Spirit, walking in the light of truth about God the Father and God the Son, are going to WANT fellowship with others. They are not only going to want total forgiveness of their sin, but they are also going to want freedom from their iniquities (their basic inbred tendencies toward sin) and from their trespasses (which are their sins against other people). Our forgiven state before God compels us to want to make things right with others. The promise of God is that the blood sacrifice of Jesus on the cross cleanses us from ALL forms of sin. It enables us to confess sin and repent of it in every area of our being—spirit, relationships, and our own soul.

Lead Your beloved one today, O Lord, into total forgiveness—of sin against You, of sin against others, and of a sin nature within. Give her warm fellowship with other believers, and a peaceful existence with total strangers!

128

Boasting Only in Christ Jesus

May it never be that I would boast, except in the cross of our Lord Jesus Christ, through which the world has been crucified to me, and I to the world.
(Galatians 6:14 NAS)

We have no reason for boasting. All of our ability, all opportunity to apply our ability, and all successful outcomes from the application of our ability are the creation and ongoing work of God in our lives! He made us, He empowers us, He renews and uses us in His service. We are altogether His project! One of God's major transformations in the life of the believer is the lack of desire to *need* acclaim from other people. The mature believer no longer compares himself or herself to others—he does not seek the trappings of fame or even the loud applause for those things that might be considered "winnings." The world's opinion no longer counts for the mature

Christian—the world has been crucified to the believer (put to death). The believer no longer *cares* what others think—only what God thinks (and thus, the believer is crucified to the world's influence). Our only reason to "boast"—which is pointing to something precious we own or a good that we have done—is to say, "I made a good decision in accepting Jesus as my Savior, and I consider my relationship with him the most precious thing any person can ever have."

Strip away from Your child, O Lord, all desire for world acclaim or approval. Give her a total focus on pleasing You.

129

Experiencing the Surpassing Greatness of God's Power

[The apostle Paul wrote:]
I pray that the eyes of your heart may be enlightened, so that you will know . . . the surpassing greatness of His power toward us who believe.
(Ephesians 1:18–19 NAS)

Many Christians do not have a very strong concept about WHO exactly is dwelling within them. The Holy Spirit that Jesus sent to dwell within all who receive Him as Savior and trust in Him as the WAY they are to live, is the *Holy Spirit of Almighty God*. This is the same Spirit that indwelled Christ Jesus. It is the same Spirit that created all things, controls all things, and has all authority over all things! His power within us is limited only by our failure to acknowledge Him, listen to Him, and trust Him. We are wise to ask the Holy Spirit to enlighten us about HIMSELF. We cannot fathom the fullness of who God wants to be in us and through us without His giving a revelation of Himself!

Heavenly Father, help Your beloved child to remember Who You are, and to trust You more. Enlighten her about Yourself!

130

Being Light in Darkness

[Jesus said:]
"Let your light shine before men in such a way that they may see your good works, and glorify your Father who is in heaven."
(Matthew 5:16 NAS)

A popular little Sunday school song in decades past said, "This little light of mine, I'm going to let it shine!" That needs to be our resolve every day of our lives. The light in us is the Light of Christ Jesus. The good works we do are extensions of His good work in us and on our behalf! The purpose of it all, is to bring glory to God the Father. Trust Jesus. Do good. Thank and praise God always. It's a way to live that even a child can understand and do!

Gracious Father, help Your child to live today in a way that brings genuine blessing to others, and evokes great praise to You.

131

Being Salt

[Jesus said:]
"You are the salt of the earth; but if the salt has become tasteless, how can it be made salty again? It is no longer good for anything, except to be thrown out and trampled under foot by men."
(Matthew 5:13 NAS)

Salt only loses its savor in one of two ways—it becomes laced with dirt or other pollutants, or it becomes watered down to the point that the salt is no longer identifiable. The metaphor extends to the spiritual realm. Sin pollutes our witness. A pursuit of favor with one's culture can lead to a watered-down life that is not discernable from the life being exhibited by those who are "in the world." God's opinion? Such a witness is WORTHLESS!

Help Your servant, today, to stay salty—to give others thirst for the truth of Christ Jesus, to be an agent of preservation for those things that are pleasing to You. Help her also to be an agent of healing for those who have been wounded by the world. Keep her free from sin. Keep her focused on You, not led astray by the world's enticements. Keep her witness totally WORTHY in Your sight!

132

Recognizing Self Deception

If anyone among you thinks he is religious, and does not bridle his tongue but deceives his own heart, this one's religion is useless. (James 1:26 NKJV)

How many times does a person blurt out a statement and then think, *Why did I say THAT? Is that REALLY what I think or believe?* Perhaps the foremost way we deceive ourselves is by *not* examining our own heart before we speak. Once we speak something we don't really believe, or know we should not believe in order to experience a renewed mind, that statement we make becomes lodged in our own memory and becomes something we "think!" It can be a vicious cycle, until eventually we DO align our thoughts and words in a negative way. And often, claim to be "religious" at the same time! To James, this is the height of hypocrisy.

Help Your servant, O Lord, to bridle her tongue by first examining her own heart to determine what she truly thinks and believes, and then to examine the situation to see if what she think and believes can impact the situation she is facing in a positive way. Give her pause before she speaks—a divine hesitation!

133

Successfully Battle the Devil

Take up the whole armor of God, that you may be able to withstand in the evil day, and having done all, to stand.
(Ephesians 6:13 NKJV)

Once we have donned the battle gear described by the apostle Paul in Ephesians 6—which is the fullness of Christ Jesus' presence and provision to us—we are required to do only two things: stand strong and pray. To stand is to display strength—it is to boldly manifest our trust in the Lord. We do not cower or withdraw from evil. We stand our ground! And we do so with thanks, praise, and petitions that God—in His ongoing faithfulness and with His all-encompassing wisdom, power, and presence—*will* accomplish His purposes! We are meant to *withstand,* which means to remain unchanged even in times of great turmoil, trouble, or pressure. God will enable us to withstand as we clothe ourselves with Christ Jesus!

Give "withstanding" power to Your child today, O Lord. Help her to stand strong in You!

Prayer is the preface to the book of Christian living, the text of the new life sermon.

—Austin Phelps

134

Willingness to Submit to Authority

Be subject to one another in the fear of Christ.
(Ephesians 5:21 NAS)

Every person is in one or more lines of authority—both within a home, as well as within a company, a city, a nation. Organization requires lines of authority for good decision-making and task-completion. In addition to matters involving law and decision-making, our "submission" often is required in matters of style and protocol. There are many methods and many styles acceptable to the Lord! Be quick to yield to other Christians in matters of style and methodology, and in matters of authority within your own body of believers. It is the only way to move forward effectively, efficiently, and in a manner pleasing to God.

Help Your beloved one, O Lord, to be willing to submit to others. Let her see that these people have been put in her "upline" for her benefit. Let her see that no matter of style or method is more important than unity within the Body of Christ.

135

Walking in Love

Walk in love, as Christ also has loved us and given Himself for us, an offering and a sacrifice to God for a sweet-smelling aroma.
(Ephesians 5:2 NKJV)

Love is not only a noun. It is a VERB. Love is manifested by GIVING. God's Word calls us to love as Christ loved—to pour out our very life's energy and substance to serve Him and to meet the needs of others around us. Such an offering of our lives is regarded as totally pleasing to God the Father.

Help Your child today, O Lord, to love You and to love others as Christ loved—with a total surrender and a total outpouring.

136

Sidestepping Pitfalls in the Pursuit of Peace

Repay no one evil for evil. Have regard for good things in the sight of all men. If it is possible, as much as depends on you, live peaceably with all men.
(Romans 12:17–18 NKJV)

At all times, we are to SEEK to live at peace with other people. We do that primarily by refusing to exact vengeance or display evil. We also do that by pointing out, uplifting, and pursuing the "good things" of life that are pleasing to God. We may not always succeed in establishing peace with another person—but as much as it "depends on us," our conscience can be clear that our intent and motivations are right. God will honor our pursuit and desire for peace.

Give Your servant a desire to live in peace with others and to sidestep the pitfalls of vengeance and anger. Show him how to put emphasis and value on the "good things" You provide and promise.

*Let our prayers, like the ancient
sacrifices, ascend morning and evening.
Let our days begin and end with God.*

—William Ellery Channing

137

Boldness in Confronting Evil

In the name of our Lord Jesus Christ, when you are gathered together, along with my spirit, with the power of our Lord Jesus Christ, deliver such a one [who has sinned grievously and without repentance] to Satan for the destruction of the flesh, that his spirit may be saved in the day of the Lord Jesus.
(1 Corinthians 5:4–5 NKJV)

The church at Corinth had experienced an incident of sexual immorality—a man taking his father's wife. Rather than confront this man and his sin, the church thought it was doing an honorable, godly thing in dismissing the severity of the sin and maintaining good fellowship with the man. The apostle Paul spoke strongly—such "glorying" in accommodating sin isn't good. He taught that "a little leaven leavens the whole lump." We always err when we think that our human accommodation of sin is a godly response; we err when we try to be more "merciful" than God, even as we err when we impart a degree of justice that is not ours to impart. God's approach is that we confront evil and call sin for what it is, that we refrain from association with an unrepentant person, and that we build up a reputation for purity within the Body of Christ. It is only when sin is confronted that it can be confessed and fully forgiven!

Give Your servant wisdom, Father, about how to love a sinner and hate a sin—about how to treat those who are unrepentant after they are confronted with their sin, and about how to offer forgiveness to those who are repentant. We cannot live with sin . . . and we cannot live without Your mercy and wisdom, O Lord!

> How deeply rooted must unbelief be in our hearts when we are surprised to find our prayer answered.
>
> —Julius Hare

138

Overcoming Evil

Do not be overcome by evil, but overcome evil with good.
(Romans 12:21 NKJV)

Evil always is pressing against us as believers in Christ Jesus. We cannot avoid the assault. How are we to respond? Not by assailing evil directly. The apostle Paul, for example, never admonished the Christians in Rome to assassinate Caesar or to engage in battle against Roman officials. Rather, we overcome evil by doing what is right in God's eyes. Our defense is our proactive OFFENSE of righteousness.

Show Your servant today, O Lord, how to engage in the acts of GOOD that will truly overthrow evil. Help him to put more points on the scoreboard for good than the devil can post for evil.

139

Willfully Choosing to Expose Unfruitful Deeds of Darkness

Do not participate in the unfruitful deeds of darkness, but instead even expose them.
(Ephesians 5:11 NAS)

We face countless intersections in life in which we can choose to participate in sinful or ungodly acts, or turn the other way. God's Word calls us to REFRAIN—no dabbling, no experimenting, no participating. Not only are we to refrain from sinful behavior, but in our refusing to participate, we are to "expose" the tricks of the devil and reveal evil for what it is. How? Perhaps the most potent way is to quote Scripture that addresses God's opinions about sin, letting

God's Word speak for itself and convict those who have a tender conscience. Scripture—plus expression of godly love—are our most powerful weapons.

Help Your servant today, O Lord, to refrain from all deeds of darkness. Give him the courage to expose those deeds with an expression of your love and Your Word.

140

Replacing a Lie with a Word of Truth

Laying aside falsehood, SPEAK TRUTH EACH ONE of you WITH HIS NEIGHBOR, for we are members of one another.
(Ephesians 4:25 NAS)

Rather than engage in conversations that are purely speculative, secular, or salacious, we are called to sidestep the lies of the devil by speaking only what is TRUTH to others—both to those who are fellow believers and those who are not. We are to refuse to engage in slander, dirty jokes and stories, rumors and gossip, and plots of evil. We are linked in a mysterious way with those to whom we "converse." We must make sure our conversations are filled with Jesus, who is the Truth.

Help Your servant today to be a purveyor of truth, and to engage in conversations that are honoring to You.

Prayer serves as an edge and border to preserve the web of life from unraveling.

—John Hall

141

Knowing When You Have Found The Pearl of Great Price

[Jesus said:]
"The kingdom of heaven is like a merchant seeking fine pearls, and upon finding one pearl of great value, he went and sold all that he had and bought it."
(Matthew 13:45–46 NAS)

In the ancient world, fine pearls were considered the most beautiful "precious stones" possible for the common man to find and purchase. Jesus reminded His followers that people often sacrificed all of their possessions in order to buy a fine pearl of great value, knowing that it was worth more than anything else they may have acquired or would ever acquire. That is the perspective we are to have regarding our relationship with Christ Jesus. Truly, nothing else matters! He is worthy of our total surrender of ALL that we are and have!

Help Your beloved child, Heavenly Father, to have a perspective that nothing in life is as valuable as having a close intimate relationship with Christ Jesus.

142

Willingness to Submit to the Holy Spirit's Guidance

[Jesus said of the Holy Spirit:]
"When He, the Spirit of truth, comes, He will guide you into all the truth; ... He will disclose to you what is to come. He will glorify Me, for He will take of Mine and disclose it to you."
(John 16:13–14 NAS)

The Holy Spirit is the Spirit of Truth. He speaks only Truth to the heart of man, confirming the Truth of God's Word (Bible) and the truth that Jesus Christ embodied. The truth has a self-fulfilling quality to it. When the truth is applied consistently to life, over time it produces an identifiable, predictable result that is good. When it is *not* applied consistently, errors and lies compound over time to produce identifiable and predictable results that are negative. In this way, as the Spirit leads us to a recognition of truth, He also presents to us a direct opportunity to define our future. We can believe and apply the truth, or we can face consequences for failing to apply the truth—consequences that God never sugar coats or hides. The Holy Spirit at all times will reveal the Truth of Jesus—not only what He said and did, but the *meaning* of His life as part of the Trinity of Holy God. We must accept it and apply it!

Gracious and loving Lord of our lives, impart Truth today!

143

Choosing to Live in Harmony with Others

Be kind to one another, tenderhearted, forgiving each other, just as God in Christ also has forgiven you.
(Ephesians 4:32 NAS)

Kindness, a tender heart, and a quickness to forgive work together in a believer's life in a synergistic way. The tender heart is more likely to be kind and to forgive. Forgiveness produces greater kindness and tenderness towards others. Kindness causes hearts to become more tender, and more likely to forgive. Jesus is our Role Model for all three of these character traits. It is out of His tender heart and divine kindness that He went to the cross to enable us to be forgiven. We are wise always to err on the side of kindness, tenderness, and forgiveness!

Heavenly Father, help Your child today to be kinder, more tenderhearted toward others—even those who are obnoxious or annoying—and to readily forgive those who trespass against her. Help her to build harmonious relationships that build up rather than tear down.

144

Recognizing the Devil at Work

[Jesus said:]
"The thief comes only to steal and kill and destroy; I came that they may have life, and have it abundantly."
(John 10:10 NAS)

Before we can effectively do battle against the devil in prayer—yes, even before we can mount an active resistance against him—we must first recognize the devil is at work and understand his purposes against us. What does the evil one seek to do? Jesus said he does three things: l)He acts to steal our possessions from us, 2) to kill our potential for winning souls (and ultimately to kill our lives), and 3) to destroy our reputation and integrity. Jesus came to defeat the devil. He promises to give us what we need, to secure our place in eternal life, to empower our witness about Him, and to maintain a sin-free reputation that is part of our wholeness (unity in thought, word, deed—body, soul, and spirit). The devil is ALL about things that limit or end life. Jesus is ALL about those things that promote and extend a fullness of life that is without equal!

Help Your child today, loving Lord, to defeat the devil by choosing to have more of Jesus in her life. Protect her, give her greater vitality than ever, and guard her steps even as you guide her along Your path for her.

Time spent in prayer is never wasted.

—Francis Fenelon

145

Being an Ambassador for Christ Jesus

[The apostle Paul wrote:]
I am an ambassador in chains.
(Ephesians 6:20 NKJV)

Paul saw himself as an ambassador for Christ Jesus and His heavenly kingdom wherever he went, even in a Roman prison. He lived according to Heaven's rules and Heaven's culture. He freely and openly told others about His *real* home. That's what ambassadors do, no matter how they are treated by the nation to which they are sent. May we see ourselves as Paul saw himself!

O Lord, You have called us to be ambassadors for our real homeland—Heaven. Help us to live according to Your rules, reflect the culture of Heaven, and to be bold in inviting others to join us in relocating to Heaven one day!

146

Living an Abundant Life

[Jesus said:]
"I have come that they may have life, and that they may have it more abundantly."
(John 10:10b NKJV)

Jesus said He came to give us life "more abundantly!" More abundantly than what? More abundantly than any form of life that the world offers, more than the abundance that any job or person can bestow upon us, more than the abundance that comes as rewards for our highest and best efforts. True abundance lies in the terms "fulfillment" and "satisfaction." We are satisfied only as we find meaning and purpose for the hours of our days. We are fulfilled only by Christ—knowing that we have done all that He has asked, for purposes that are far beyond ourselves. It is to Christ that we must go with our request, "Show me what You want me to do. Impart *Your* meaning to my life."

I ask today, O Lord, that You reveal to Your child an even stronger understanding that You alone are the One who gives meaning to life and a fulfillment to purpose. Help her to walk in Your ways only, to bring glory to Your name only, and thus fulfill her destiny on this earth.

147

Being Strong in the Lord

Be strong in the Lord and in the power of His might.
(Ephesians 6:10 NKJV)

How strong is the Lord? He is the Almighty, omnipotent God, fully in control of all things and capable of accomplishing all that He wills. Our strength does not lie in ourselves—not even the strength of our faith. Our strength lies solely in our relationship with the Lord. We must wrap ourselves up in Him, completely enrobing ourselves in His identity. Then, and only then, do we have the authority and ability He has promised to impart to those who are His disciples.

Grant, O Lord, a new insight to Your beloved about what it means to be strong. Help Your child to rely more and more upon You for the enduring power and resolve to live out Your life on this earth today.

Prayer is the wing wherewith the
soul flies to heaven.

—Bishop Ambrose of Milan

148

Praying for All the Saints with Perseverance

Praying always with all prayer and supplication in the Spirit, being watchful to this end with all perseverance and supplication for all the saints.
(Ephesians 6:18 NKJV)

Prayer is making petition. It is asking God for something. Supplication is the *attitude* we are to have when we pray—an attitude of humble appeal to Someone who has the power to grant what we request. The apostle Paul told the Ephesians to make their petitions with an attitude of supplication —and to make petitions according to the Spirit's directing, with perseverance, and for all who are the redeemed followers of Christ Jesus.

Help Your child today, dear Father, to come to you in humility that You alone are capable of answering all petitions in a way that results in earthly blessing and eternal reward. Help Your child to listen closely to the Spirit, so that her petitions are already in alignment with what You want to do. Help her to persevere in her prayers, watching always for Your answers.

149

Fruitfulness

[Jesus said:]
"By this My Father is glorified, that you bear much fruit; so you will be My disciples."
(John 15:8 NKJV)

Not all those who "followed" Jesus became true disciples of Jesus. Some "followed" out of curiosity, seeking to see miracles and hear new teachings. Some "followed" to be part of the crowd. Those who truly became disciples were those who began to LIVE according to what they had heard and seen. The same is true for us today. A disciple is a real "student" who not only learns theory, but also practices application. The sign that a believer has moved from being an observer to a disciple is the bearing of spiritual fruit—both in character and in deeds. Jesus said, "By the bearing of fruit, God is glorified"—not merely by giving ascent to a doctrine or associating with other believers.

Help Your servant, Father, to become a true disciple of Jesus Christ. Help him to learn Christ, and to apply what he learns to bring glory to Your name!

150

Standing Firm in the Face of Severe Persecution

Put on the whole armor of God, that you may be able to stand against the wiles of the devil.
(Ephesians 6:11 NKJV)

The devil is at war against every believer. It doesn't matter what the believer does or doesn't do, or how faithful or mature the believer might be. The devil wages war! We are in a defensive position. Our offense is never to *fight* the devil, but rather, to win souls by the witness of our lives and our words. It is our offense that is what defeats the devil. It is our offense that also prompts the devil's assaults against us. All persecution comes ultimately from the devil—people may be used by the devil, but the force behind the persecution is always the force of evil. To stand firm in the face of persecution, therefore, is to recognize the source of the persecution and the purpose for it. And then, we must put on the fullness of Christ's character and STAND firm, refusing to cave, compromise, or cower before the devil's assaults. Praise God in the face of persecution; pray for persistence and endurance. And, look for God to win the victory!

Help Your child, O Lord, to understand the reason behind all the hard times and troubles he is facing—the real reason that goes far beyond anything Your beloved child has done or failed to do. Help him to see the big picture of the devil as his enemy. Help him to put on Christ and stand firm today!

151

Rewards

If anyone's work which he has built on it endures, he will receive a reward.
(1 Corinthians 3:14 NKJV)

The Bible refers to God as a Rewarder of those who diligently seek Him. (Hebrews 11:6) God rewards primarily with His presence. When we do what He desires for us to do, He blesses our work with a reward that is only partially for this earth. The bulk of our reward always lies in heaven. The reward of God is as sure as the presence of God—it *will* be given—and it will be as eternal as God Himself.

Give Your child a glimpse of the tremendous reward that comes from knowing You and obeying You—the ultimate reward is more of You! Nothing could be greater. Assure Your beloved one of that truth today, I pray.

> The sweetest lesson I have learned in God's school is to let the Lord choose for me.
>
> —D. L. Moody

152

Citizenship in the Kingdom of Heaven

Ye are no more strangers and foreigners, but fellowcitizens with the saints, and of the household of God.
(Ephesians 2:19 KJV)

Few things are more motivating, or hopeful, than a strong remembrance that we are, ultimately, citizens of the kingdom of Heaven! All things can be endured on this earth because all things of this earth are temporary and passing. Our true home is Heaven and until that day, we can take comfort and joy that we are part of a worldwide community of people who love the Lord Jesus Christ—in other words, the Church universal. We are not estranged from God. We are in relationship with Him and a part of His household. What cause to rejoice and to persevere in walking according to His commandments!

Give Your child today a new assurance that her name is written among the citizenship rolls in Heaven! Impart to her the hope and renewing strength associated with her citizenship in Heaven—with You and for ever.

153

Comfort in Times of Mourning

[Jesus taught:]
Blessed are those who mourn,
For they shall be comforted.
(Matthew 5:4 NKJV)

"Mourn" is a term always related to *loss*. It may be the loss of a loved one, loss of a personal sense of contribution or worthiness, or a loss of relationship. The opposite of mourn is GAIN—and Jesus promises that He can and will more than compensate for anything we lose. He has for us an everlasting increase, an eternal prize, and the abiding presence of Himself.

Please whisper, Father, Your comforting words to Your beloved child, assuring her that You are with her always, and that she is valuable, worthy, and acceptable in your sight. Assure her that You are in control of all things, and that even though she may not understand Your plans and purpose, You *do* have a plan for using even this sad and painful time for Your eternal purposes and her eternal benefit. You will replace with Your own self anything she feels she has lost!

154

Being a Peacemaker

[Jesus taught:]
"Blessed are the peacemakers,
For they shall be called sons of God."
(Matthew 5:9 NKJV)

Peacemakers are ultimately those who bring about reconciliation between God and man. The person who does this is truly a child following in the footsteps of his or her Heavenly Father. Along the way, of course, we have abundant opportunities to bring about reconciliation between people, which very often begins as a truce (generally the first step in many peace-making processes). We must be aware, however, that when we are pursuing peace between God and man, we will likely face opposition from the person who needs peace with God. When we are pursuing peace between two people or two groups, we are likely going to face opposition from *both* people or groups. Everybody wants peace on their terms, but not everybody wants peace on God's terms!

Help Your child today, O Lord, to be a true peacemaker, bringing someone into closer relationship with You. Give her strength to be a person who seeks peace in the church, a full reconciliation among all true believers.

155

Giving Up a Desire for Vengeance

Never take your own revenge, beloved, but leave room for the wrath of God, for it is written, "VENGEANCE IS MINE, I WILL REPAY," says the Lord.
(Romans 12:19 NAS)

Every person, it seems, has a secret desire that something bad should happen, at least to some degree, to those who have hurt them or caused them loss. God says to leave their punishment to Him. Only God sees the fullness of His plan and purpose for the hurtful person, and only God knows fully their motives and desires that may reflect deep inner pain that only God can heal. When we step in, we thwart or limit God's work. Even more than the challenge to refrain from revenge is the concept that we give up a *desire* to take revenge. That is true love, and it is the kind of love that leads a person to forgive (release a person from personal judgment and condemnation). When we give up an emotional desire for vengeance, God can then give us an emotional desire to be a blessing—a much better use of emotional energy!

Help Your servant, Heavenly Father, to allow YOU to be his Defender and Victor. Help him to release any thoughts of revenge and feelings of hatred to you. Show him how to be Your agent of blessing rather than a self-appointed agent of wrath.

156

Leaving a Godly Inheritance

A good man leaves an inheritance to his children's children.
(Proverbs 13:22 NKJV)

The godly parent is not only concerned about the wellbeing of his children, but also that what he gives to his children is worthy to be passed on to his grandchildren! The godly inheritance is first and foremost *spiritual* in nature. It is a passing on of the commands of God, the love of God, the promises of God, and the provisions of mercy and forgiveness made possible by Christ Jesus. It is a passing on of all that we know as justice, righteousness, and virtue.

Help Your child today, to leave a godly inheritance to her children and grandchildren. Show her the riches that truly matter, and reveal to her how she can pass these on to future generations in her family, as well as to those who are her "children" in You.

157

Spiritual Eyes that See

[Jesus said:]
"Do you not yet perceive nor understand? . . . Having eyes, do you not see?"
(Mark 8:17–18 NKJV)

A popular cultural phrase proclaims, "There's more than meets the eye." In truth, even when we perceive something with great clarity and in great detail, we can often miss the *meaning* of what we are seeing. All events and phenomena convey a *message* from God, even those things we have come to see as routine or mundane.

Communication is occurring, but we may not be receiving all that the Sender is broadcasting. Ask God to give you spiritual eyes to see what He is doing on the earth, and to understand His purposes and His goals.

O Lord, open the spiritual eyes of Your servant so he might not only perceive and see what is happening around him, through him, and to him . . . but have a glimpse into Your purposes. Show him that all things bear spiritual meaning.

158

Spiritual Ears to Hear

[Jesus said:]
"He who enters by the door is a shepherd of the sheep. To him the doorkeeper open, and the sheep hear his voice, and he calls his own sheep by name and leads them out. When he puts forth all his own, he goes ahead of them, and the sheep follow him because they know his voice."
(John 10:2–4 NAS)

Many people are intent on hearing the latest news, the latest chart-topping music, the latest gossip, the latest poll results. The list goes on. In truth, the only thing we truly NEED to hear, on a daily basis, is the voice of the Lord, calling to us so that we might follow in His footsteps and do the work that we see Him already in the process of doing. Our Shepherd calls us personally, and He leads us, by continuing speaking to us, until we arrive at a place where we experience the fullness of His provision (our personalized green pastures and still waters). It is our responsibility to stay close enough to the Shepherd to hear His voice, avoiding any detours or slothfulness, and to listen closely for His voice. He is speaking! That is not the issue. The issue is whether we are listening.

Gracious Shepherd, help Your beloved lamb to hear Your voice and be quick to follow in Your footsteps.

159

Unity of Faith

He Himself gave some to be apostles, some prophets, some evangelists, and some pastors and teachers, for the equipping of the saints, for the work of ministry, for the edification of the body of Christ, till we all come to the unity of the faith and of the knowledge of the Son of God, to a perfect man, to the measure of the stature of the fullness of Christ.
(Ephesians 4:11–13 NKJV)

The Bible does *not* call us to uniformity, which is every person being exactly alike. The Bible does *not* call us to a unified set of design or protocol specs. Rather, God calls us to unity, which is agreement on a set of values or beliefs. Our foremost areas for agreement are to be a unity of the faith (the essentials of our faith), and to a common understanding that Jesus is the Son of God. This passage follows the apostle Paul's reminder that "there is one body and one Spirit" . . . one hope . . . one Lord, one faith, one baptism, one God and Father of all. (See Ephesians 4:4–6.) It is under the umbrella of unity in belief that God has given each person a specific work to do and a role to fill. (See Ephesians 4:7.)

Father, I pray today that Your beloved child will stay focused on what is truly important for eternity—the message of Jesus Christ and the faith imparted to the Church. Keep her from detours, or from straying into concerns with those things that are not central to the evangelism of the lost or the growth of Your saints on the earth. Show her how to use the gifts You have imparted to her to bring glory to Your name, ALWAYS.

160

Fully Embracing the Identity of "God's Child"

For you are all sons of God through faith in Christ Jesus.
(Galatians 3:26 NAS)

What an awesome and compelling truth that we who believe in Christ Jesus are the fully adopted children of God! The Lord certainly loves all of His creation, but not all people choose to accept God's offer of "sonship" through Jesus Christ. Those who do sometimes fail to grasp the fullness of the inheritance and privileges that are theirs—not for self-promotion, but for the furtherance of God's kingdom on this earth. We must not fail to embrace our responsibility—the furtherance of God's kingdom for *His* glory. We must not lose sight that we will live with our Father forever in the perfection of Heaven.

Give Your child a new insight into the truth that he is Your son, Your heir, Your beloved child—now and forever!

161

Being in Position to Be Blessed

"I will bless you ... so you shall be a blessing."
(Genesis 12:2 NAS)

The purpose of God's blessings in our lives is not that we grow richer, more famous, or gain more power over others. We are to be a conduit of blessing! The blessings we receive are blessings we are to pass along. God has more than sufficient reward for all who will turn to Him. His blessings are unlimited ... if we don't try to hoard them. Hoarding only stops the flow of increase in our lives.

Make Your servant an instrument of Your blessing today, O Lord!

162

A Willingness to Pray for Persecutors and Enemies

[Jesus taught:]
"Love your enemies, bless those who curse you, do good to those who hate you, and pray for those who spitefully use you and persecute you, that you may be sons of your Father in heaven."
(Matthew 5:44–45 NKJV)

Jesus gave us very clear instructions about how we are to deal with four classes of people who stand in opposition to us. When it comes to our enemies—those who seek to undermine, thwart, or destroy us: we are to give to them. When it comes to those who curse us, we are to bless them! When it comes to those who hate us: we are to do good to them. When it comes to those who seek to use us in spiteful (petty and malicious) ways, and to those who persecute us (saying or doing things designed to hurt us): we are to pray for them. In each instance, we are to do the exact *opposite* of what those who are against us are likely to expect! Our enemies are looking for a fight—we are to give them kindness. Those who curse us are expecting a verbal war—we are to give them a blessing. Those who hate us are expecting us to respond with hate—we are to give them something good. Those who use us and persecute us are expecting us to use and persecute them—we give them prayer. What we sow is what we will reap. In sowing good, we *will* reap reward.

Help Your child today, O Lord to rise above the behavior of those who oppose her and to give them what they do NOT deserve—an extension of Your mercy, kindness, love, and goodness.

Prayer is profitable wherever it is invested.

—Anonymous

163

Producing Excellence

Earnestly desire the best gifts. And yet I show you a more excellent way.
(1 Corinthians 12:31 NKJV)

In all things, we are to do our best, expecting God's best help, God's best outcome, God's best rewards. God surpasses all excellence—He is PERFECTION. And while no human being can ever achieve perfection, we can do our utmost, giver our best effort, and aim for the highest and most noble goals. Above all, we are to desire the best gifts that God bestows, and have a willingness to use those gifts to bless others. The more excellent way that the apostle Paul described for the Corinthians was LOVE—the pure, unadultered love of God, poured out in generous and faithful ways. Love is the best we can give!

Help Your child today to do her best, and honor You in every way possible.

164

A Supply that Meets Whatever Is Lacking

The LORD said to Moses, "Behold, I will rain bread from heaven for you."
(Exodus 16:5 NKJV)

God meets the needs of His beloved children! His ability to provide is infinite and everlasting. Does this mean that God supplies ALL that we "desire?" Only if our desire is a part of Heaven's plan and purpose for us. What is lacking in our lives is usually not "stuff," but rather, spiritual substance. Only Christ Jesus can provide for that kind of lack.

Help Your beloved child today, O Lord, to see that her needs are primarily "more of Jesus." Supply her true needs. Alter her list of wants to conform to Your list of what You want for her.

> *The simple heart that freely asks in love, obtains.*
>
> —John Greenleaf Whittier

165

Treasure Stored Up in Heaven

[Jesus said:]
"If you want to be perfect, go, sell what you have and give to the poor, and you will have treasure in heaven; and come, follow Me." (Matthew 19:21 NKJV)

We tend to think of treasure as wealth—various forms of precious items that can be used in "exchanges" of various types (buying and selling, bartering, giving with expectation of receiving). The Bible meaning of the word is nearly always related to things of tremendous VALUE, including things greatly loved. What we have in the way of material substance must always be evaluated according to value, and in what ways we might "exchange" our treasure to bring about eternal rewards and benefits to others. Anything we give away on earth in exchange for the Gospel to be advanced is not lost. It morphs into everlasting treasure in God's home.

Reveal to Your beloved one, O Lord, the true meaning of treasure. Show her ways you desire for her to give her treasure to benefit others, and in so doing, amass treasure in Heaven. Inspire her to be a giver of what You have given to her!

166

Sure Footing

The LORD God is my strength;
He will make my feet like deer's feet,
And He will make me walk on my high hills.
(Habakkuk 3:19 NKJV)

The mountain areas of Israel throughout the nation's history have been regarded as places of escape and refuge. The craggy "trails" are often very narrow, hugging ledges with steep drop-offs. The ibex are perfectly suited for that terrain, and they are abundant in many areas. Note that the prophet Habakkuk says that, as we trust God for HIS strength, God will give us the sure footing of the ibex, and He will enable us to walk on OUR high hills—the highest reaches of our potential and God-given purpose! God always calls us upward, not merely forward. He provides the high hills as our place of purpose and protection. He calls us to HIKE toward Heaven, not just amble on easy, level, paved surfaces.

Give strength, O Lord, to Your servant today. Help him to maintain his balance in You. Give him ability to reach his full potential and the purpose You have planned for him.

167

A Desire to Walk Worthy of the Lord

[We] do not cease to pray for you . . . that you may walk worthy of the Lord, fully pleasing to Him, being fruitful in every good work and increasing in the knowledge of God.
(Colossians 1:8,10 NKJV)

What an amazing thing to be made aware of God's great love, be forgiven of sin, be restored to full relationship with God the Father, and to receive the Holy Spirit as imparted by Christ Jesus! And what an awesome responsibility to walk in a way that is worthy of a relationship with Almighty God! Not that we can attain "worth" on our own, but rather, that *God* says we are worthy to be called His sons and daughters on the basis of what Jesus did on the Cross and what the Holy Spirit does in our lives daily. God is *always* the One who makes us worthy. He is the One who enables us to be fully pleasing to Him, to be fruitful as we do good, and Who reveals more and more of Himself to us as we live out our faith.

Lord, help Your child today to do all that is pleasing to you, and to accept the awesome truth that YOU regard Your child as "worthy" of Your presence, Your love, Your calling, You life-imparting fruitfulness. Help Your beloved to feel Your pleasure and to respond to You with steadfast faithfulness.

168

Good Works that Bear Good Fruit

. . . being fruitful in every good work.
(Colossians 1:10 NKJV)

Good works are "good" if God says they are good; they are necessary only if God says they are necessary; and they produce eternal fruit and earthly blessing only if God causes the fruitbearing. A farmer can do everything in his power to plant the best seed in the best soil, and tend a plant the best he knows how. But only God produces a harvest. God will not do our part. We cannot do His part. Trust God to produce fruit in your life, and through your life.

Help Your child today, O Lord, to pursue those things that You call good and necessary, and to do all in his realm of ability to plant the best seeds of time, money, and talent into the best soil. Help him to trust You to do Your part—turn a tiny seed into a mighty harvest.

169

Growing in Knowledge of the Lord

For this reason also, since the day we heard of it, we have not ceased to pray for you, and to ask that you may be filled with the knowledge of His will in all spiritual wisdom and understanding . . . increasing in the knowledge of God.
(Colossians 1:9–10 NAS)

It is one thing to know *about* God, and a very different thing to *know* God directly, personally, and with increasing spiritual intimacy. To know God one must spend time with God—listening intently to His voice and asking for His directions from His Word. It also means being willing to be totally transparent before God. No issue is too difficult, no mystery too profound, no sin too great to talk to God about it! Genuine transparency and vulnerability put a person into the prime position to *experience* God's love and forgiveness—not just to know about these traits of God in the abstract, but to *experience* them as reality in one's deepest core.

Give Your servant a desire to know You better. Wrap Your loving arms around her today, and give her a divine assurance of Your presence with her at all times.

> We possess a divine artillery that
> silences the enemy and inflicts upon him
> the damage he would inflict upon us.
>
> —Corrie ten Boom

170

Quickness to Apologize

"Please forgive the trespass of your servant."
(1 Samuel 25:28 NKJV)

In the Bible, a woman named Abigail had a husband who made a serious error in judgment that put Abigail, her maidservants, and her entire household in danger. She went to David, to whom the wrong had been committed, and asked him for forgiveness. Her quickness in sending an apology and providing the substance that David requested, averted death, as well as kept David's record clear when it came to killing Israelites. Her apology also paved the way for her later to marry David! We are always wise to try to be a bridge of reconciliation between those who are at odds. We are always wise to be quick to apologize for wrongs in which we have played a part.

Give Your servant a heart eager to apologize and set things right with others—even in cases where he may be right! Give him a greater desire for peace than a desire to be in control. Give him the courage to apologize directly, not simply to think "I'm sorry" thoughts.

171

The Protection of God's Angels

Are they [God's angels] not all ministering spirits sent forth to minister for those who will inherit salvation?
(Hebrews 1:14 NKJV)

The angels of God do His bidding—and in the Bible, as well as in history, God has sent His angels to protect and provide for His people, often in amazing ways. We are not in a position to summon angels, nor are we to seek to communicate directly with them, but we can ask God to use *whatever* means He desires to help us when we are in need or danger. We should not be surprised if our help comes in unexpected and awe-inspiring ways . . . very possibly the work of His unseen ministering spirits!

Give Your child the faith to believe that You have all resources available to help him and to supply his "unmet" needs or resolve his "unsolvable" problems. Give him an appreciation for Your supernatural power, and at the same time, utter reliance upon You to send *Your* answers according to *Your* timing and Your methods to bring about a greater expression of *Your* glory!

172

Overcoming the Iniquities of the Fathers

Hide Your face from my sins,
And blot out all my iniquities.
(Psalm 51:9 NKJV)

Sins are the attitudes we harbor and the things we do that cause estrangement or separation in our relationship with God—they are breaches of His commandments. Iniquities are generally linked in the Scripture to one's "fathers" or ancestors. Our ancestors have given us both DNA that has embedded within it a propensity to sin in certain ways. Our ancestors have also given us "habits"— generational ways of thinking, believing, and acting that are passed down to us by their role modeling of various behaviors and their communication of various values. Science is just now discovering the many ways in which generational habits are coded into DNA. The good news is that we do NOT automatically need to behave as our forefathers did or do. We do NOT need to repeat bad patterns. We can exercise our gift of free will from God the Father to make new choices and new decisions to live according to God's Word, not according to man's example, even if it is part of our genome.

Dear Father, help Your child today to recognize the iniquities that have been passed on to her from her forefathers. Help her to rely upon You to change those habitual ways of thinking and responding to life. Give her a deep desire to reverse those things that are negative as the result of genetic or role-modeling influences. Free her from her inherited iniquities!

> *By far the most important thing about praying is to keep at it.*
>
> —Frederick Buechner

173

Refusing to Trip Over or Be a Stumblingblock

"Take the stumbling block out of the way of My people."
(Isaiah 57:14b NKJV)

Stumbling blocks refer most often in the Bible to iniquities—sins that tend to run from generation to generation—or to customs that are more prohibitive of behavior than protective of one's soul. In the natural world, a stumbling block was often the stonework at the entrance to a home—intended to block unwanted pests, dirt, or water from entering a home. If a person didn't watch his step upon entering or leaving, he could trip easily. The point is—we must examine all things that have the potential to "trip us up." We also must examine all attitudes and behaviors in our lives that might trip up others. Make straight and clear the way of the Lord!

O Lord, help Your beloved one today to see all the obstacles in her path and to avoid tripping over any of them. Don't let her be an obstacle to others in their walk with Christ.

174

Refraining from Even the Appearance of Evil

Abstain from all appearance of evil.
(1 Thessalonians 5:22 KJV)

Our culture today has a very high threshold of tolerance for the appearance of evil. We claim, of course, to hate evil and to oppose it. But we readily tolerate innumerable acts of violence, immorality, and various forms of conniving, manipulation, hatred, and vengeance, especially in the public media. We consume thousands upon thousands of acts of evil "vicariously"—including news reports that portray real-time crime. All of this pollutes the soul. It dulls our senses and creates a dangerous apathy. Another way to express the apostle Paul's words to the Thessalonians might be: "Don't even look at evil from afar! Your vicarious participation not only damages you, but your witness for Christ and your reputation as a whole."

Lord, help Your beloved today to *desire* to abstain from all appearance of evil. Let there be no vicarious dabbling or voyeurism in things that are distasteful to You!

175

A Desire to Study God's Word

"This book of the law shall not depart from your mouth, but you shall meditate on it day and night, so that you may be careful to do according to all that is written in it; for then you will make your way prosperous, and then you will have success."
(Joshua 1:8 NAS)

One of the meanings of the word "meditate" in Hebrew is "mutter." We are to hear the Word of God, commit it to memory, and recite it often—indeed, continually! In this way the Word of God becomes our way of *thinking*. The voicing of God's Word engraves it into our mental processing. The Word becomes our framework for making choices and decisions. It becomes the backdrop for our understanding of ALL the world around us.

Lord, help Your beloved child today to read, hear, learn, and memorize Your Word, and then to voice it often all day, and into the evening hours before bedtime. Forge her thought processes in alignment with Your truth, I pray.

176

Diligence

Be diligent to present yourself approved to God as a workman who does not need to be ashamed, accurately handling the word of truth. (2 Timothy 2:15 NAS)

Diligence is the persistent application of effort to accomplish something or fulfill something. It involves learning, practicing, and applying. That is the way we are to approach God's Word. We are to make a concerted effort to learn it and apply it faithfully, with steadfastness and persistence. There is nothing easy about *applying* God's Word to one's daily life. Head knowledge is acquired rather easily. Life application is a matter that involves ongoing effort!

Help Your child today, dear Heavenly Father, to be diligent in her study and application of Your commandments. Give her persistence and a willingness to exert the effort necessary to live a Christ-honoring life.

177

Freedom from Shame and False Guilt

Do not hide Your face from Your servant,
For I am in distress; answer me quickly.
Oh draw near to my soul and redeem it;
Ransom me because of my enemies!
You know my reproach and my shame and dishonor;
All my adversaries are before You.
(Psalm 69:17–19 NAS)

"Reproach" involves disgrace or criticism from others for something that you have done wrong, and you know you have erred or sinned. "Shame" involves feelings of dishonor, embarrassment, or unworthiness—it is a "comparative" emotion. We are made to feel shame when we weigh our failures against the seeming perfection of others, or when others accuse us of being less than perfect. "Dishonor" involves a loss of respect or reputation in the eyes of others, as the result of their being informed of your sin or error. All three—reproach, shame, and dishonor—create distress in us. All three are very often the tools of our enemies, who seek to put us in a position of ill repute. All three cause us to hang our heads. They are emotions that slow our progress, diminish our sense of value and worthiness, and cause us to cower in the presence of our accusers. We are wise to take these emotions to God and ask Him to deliver us—to forgive us, restore us, and create a new level of God-esteems-us confidence.

Free Your beloved one, I pray, O Lord, from all feelings of reproach, shame, and dishonor. Let her walk freely and boldly in the light of Your forgiveness and the value that You extend to her by Your presence!

> *Holy, humble, penitent, believing, earnest, persevering prayer is never lost; it always prevails.*
>
> *—Weeks magazine*

178

Overcoming the Lust of the Flesh

For all that is in the world, the lust of the flesh and the lust of the eyes and the boastful pride of life, is not from the Father, but is from the world.
(1 John 2:16 NAS)

Lustful thoughts can strike us at any time. They are the impulses that drive—compel, almost force—us to seek satisfaction of our basic needs for food, water, sex, and other physical and natural necessities. Lusts are related to this world—to this temporal earthly life. They are not a part of eternity. We must recognize that what strikes us as tempting on earth has a short shelf life!

Give Your child the ability to overcome the lust of the flesh today. Help her to keep her eyes on You and on the eternal life that lies ahead.

179

Overcoming the Lust of the Eyes

[Jesus said:]
"If your eye causes you to stumble, pluck it out and throw it from you. It is better for you to enter life with one eye, than to have two eyes and be cast into the fiery hell."
(Matthew 18:9 NAS)

The lust of the eyes (see 1 John 2:16) is nearly always associated with envy and greed—it is a wanting of things that are not rightfully ours or that are beyond our basic needs. We crave possessions, in part, because we use them to define our own worthiness. The sad truth, according to Jesus, is that our envy and greed can cause us to become root-bound in this world's systems, our eyes focused on the here and now rather than on God's eternal values and truth. We are better to cast away—GIVE AWAY—our excess possessions with generosity in order to keep our focus on what truly matters.

Free Your child today, O Lord, from selfishness, envy, and greed. Show her how to give away what is keeping her from having a clear sightline to Heaven.

> I know not by what methods rare,
> but this I know: God answers prayer.
>
> —Eliza M. Hickok

180

Overcoming the Pride of Life

Pride goes before destruction,
And a haughty spirit before stumbling.
(Proverbs 16:18 NAS)

The pride of life (see 1 John 2:16) is a desire for fame and recognition. The person filled with pride sees only "me, myself, and I," and he needs constant affirmation and accolades to feel he has genuine value. He needs for others to esteem him before he can esteem himself. God's plan is for us to draw our worthiness—all value and esteem—from who HE says we are, His beloved child and the inheritor of His riches in Christ Jesus. Those who see only themselves usually trip over their own feet. Those who see others and seek to reach out to them with God's love, walk with purpose.

Help Your servant today, dear Lord, to respond to life with concern for others, and a deep desire to affirm and encourage others. Help him to draw his own sense of value directly from You, not from human beings.

181

Marital Fidelity

Enjoy life with the woman whom you love all the days of your fleeting life which He has given to you under the sun.
(Ecclesiastes 9:9a NAS)

God desires for people to make a wise choice in marriage, and then to make an ongoing wise choice to stay married. Love is not only a warm affectionate emotion; it is demonstrated by "giving." If we lose the "feelings" of love, we can nearly always reclaim them by ongoing giving of prayer, kindness, and generous genuine praise for the good attitudes, beliefs, and behavior of the other person. When we "give" we boost our own joy in life, knowing we have done what is godly and productive, even if we don't see immediate results from our giving. Ongoing marital fidelity is *possible*, but it requires a generous heart willing to give sacrificially and to stay committed even when emotions fluctuate.

Help Your servant today in her marriage. Help her to stay faithful to the vows she made to love, honor, and cherish her spouse. Work on her spouse in a similar manner to stay faithful to her!

182

Refusing to Engage in Idle Speculation or Gossip

Refuse foolish and ignorant speculations, knowing that they produce quarrels.
(2 Timothy 2:23 NAS)

No project or work of godly value occurs in the presence of ongoing "speculation" or gossip. Speculation asks questions, but never produces definitive or trustworthy answers. Gossip casts doubt on a person's ability to be trusted or held in esteem. Both speculation and gossip create confusion, not clarity. Confusion nearly always devolves into frustration, anger, and quarreling. Stay on the side of truth and honor!

Help Your beloved servant to turn a deaf ear to idle speculation and gossip. Keep him focused on the work and goals You have set before him. Let him speak only words of truth that build up and do not tear down, that produce clear vision and not cloudy confusion.

183

Paying No Attention to Myths and Old-Wives' Tales

Nor give heed to fables and endless genealogies, which cause disputes rather than godly edification.
(1 Timothy 1:4 NKJV)

The ancient world relied heavily on stories of favor and deliverance at the hands of mythical gods, who were thought to rule over all happenstance—"luck," in other words. The ancient world also placed extreme value on one's ancestry, more so than on one's personal character or deeds, even to the point of believing that certain people were destined (apart from anything they did) to a life of riches or poverty. The apostles strongly opposed both positions. They taught that God alone governs all circumstance, and because He controls all things, He can work all things to good for all who obey Him. They also taught personal responsibility, and the need for personal confession and repentance. It is only when a person takes responsibility for his own attitudes and actions, and confesses his own sins to God, that true forgiveness and spiritual empowerment can occur.

Do not face a day until you have faced God.

—Unknown

Help Your child today, O Lord, to take stock of his own life and to see that You require humble confession and repentance. Show him that he cannot count on the abuse or blessings of parents or other ancestors as an excuse in Your eyes. Show him that You alone are behind anything that might be called a co-incidence. Help him to lay aside all false beliefs and trust only in You!

184

Modesty

Likewise, I want women to adorn themselves with proper clothing, modestly and discreetly, not with braided hair and gold or pearls or costly garments, but rather by means of good works, as is proper for women making a claim to godliness.
(1 Timothy 2:9 NAS)

The Bible's approach to "adornment" was one of moderation. Many women in the Roman world dressed solely to draw attention to themselves for the purpose of seducing men or of pride-filled attempts to gain greater social status and the power and fame associated with that status. They dressed, did their hair, and wore their jewels as a means of self-identity. They saw these outer displays associated with "image," as a display of their worth and value. This should not be the attitude or behavior of the believer, wrote the apostle Paul. He encouraged Christian women to see their identity solely in Christ and to adorn themselves in a way that called attention to Him, not to themselves. Appearance was not equated with value or worthiness—rather, "good works" done in the name of the Lord and for the furtherance of the Gospel on the earth. True worth and value are bestowed only by the Lord. You cannot buy worthiness, nor can you put it on. Value flows from the inside out.

Help Your child today, O Lord, to see that worth and value cannot be gained by what one wears or how one "looks." Free her from feeling that she must "keep up appearance" and let her focus on the things that truly matter to You!

> *If one draw near to God with praise and prayer even half a cubit, God will go twenty leagues to meet him.*
>
> —Sir Edwin Arnold

185

Moderation

Let your moderation be known unto all men.
(Philippians 4:5 KJV)

Moderation is manifested by self-limiting, or self-control. The concept of moderation exists only because some things are so exciting or so enticing that we begin to think, "if one is good, two is better, and three is even better than two!" That can be true for things that are good for us, as well as things that are bad for us. Anything that takes on a degree of excessive indulgence can exert an addictive power over our lives, to the point that we begin to seek satisfaction of our lusts rather than to engage in godly activities that benefit others. Truly, a life focused on meeting the needs of self (expecting full satisfaction, in any area of life) becomes a life that cannot be simultaneously focused on God's purposes or the fulfillment of God's plans. The apostle Paul wrote to Christians living in a world of Roman excess. He said, "Your moderation will be a strong witness that you do not live for yourself, but for the Lord."

Give Your child a good "braking system," O Lord. Help her to say "no" to any impulse to live a life of self-focused self-gratification. Make her mindful of the needs of others. Give her the ability to resist the temptations associated with lusts of the flesh, lusts of the eyes, and the pride of life.

186

Having a Spirit of Love, Power, and a Sound Mind

For God has not given us a spirit of timidity, but of power and love and discipline.
(2 Timothy 1:7 NAS)

God does not desire that any of His beloved children be paralyzed by fear. He has imparted the Holy Spirit to those who believe in Christ Jesus! Is the Holy Spirit weak? No. He is omnipotent. Is the Holy Spirit unloving? No. He is the comforter. Is the Holy Spirit without purpose or constraining power? No. He is always actively at work seeking to guide us in the right paths that are for our eternal reward and earthly benefit! Power is the ability to get things done, love is the attitude we are to have at all times—the things we "give" to the world with love are our work. Discipline is the steadfast focus required to accomplish things that are beyond the moment. We are to actively rely upon the Holy Spirit to impart His power, love, and discipline to us daily.

Give Your beloved servant more of Your power, Your love, and Your discipline today, O Lord. I pray that he will walk boldly, confident that what He cannot do in his own strength, You can do. Help Him to love others as You love, and to be steadfast and steady in all his thoughts and deeds, just as You are steadfast and utterly trustworthy at all times.

187

The Miracle Embedded in Today

Moses said to the people, "Do not fear! Stand by and see the salvation of the LORD which He will accomplish for you today."
(Exodus 14:13a NAS)

God has a miracle for every person every day—maybe more than one! A miracle is simply an act of God that is "beyond" anything a human being or circumstances alone can produce. God is active in the world, and especially so in the life of the believer in Christ Jesus. We fail to receive all of God's "miracles" that are flowing to us because we aren't looking for them! Why? In some cases, because we aren't looking for God's activity in us, through us, and around us. Doubt, fear, and simple lackadaisical "floating along in life" behavior keep us from seeing the wonders of God at work.

Help Your child today, O Lord, to be mindful of You in her daily life. Do not let her mind be shrouded by fear or doubt. Do not let her get so caught up in the normal activities of practical daily living that she fails to see the world with spiritual eyes. Open her entire being to experience You in every facet of her life and day.

188

A Sufficiency of Grace

[The apostle Paul wrote:]
But by the grace of God I am what I am, and His grace toward me did not prove vain.
(1 Corinthians 15:10 NAS)

God's work in us (His grace) is always life-transforming. His grace is a package of infinite love, mercy, favor, and goodwill—it is at all times wrapped in forgiveness and is a reflection of God's own excellence, authority, and sufficiency. We must be quick to acknowledge that we are what God has made us to be—and that, to the degree that our lives are making an impact for the Gospel, we are who we allow God to *use* us to be. When God is fully in charge, and we recognize, we cannot fail because He cannot fail. Even if we do not appear to be winning, according to our own definition or the definition of others, we *are* winning if we are trusting Him to work in us and through us. His plans do not fail.

Give Your beloved one a strong sense of Your sufficiency today. Help him to rely totally on You to make and mold him, then fill him and use him for Your purposes. Give him insights as to what it really means to be successful from *Your* perspective.

189

Good Cash Flow

[The apostle Paul wrote:]
I have received everything in full and have an abundance; I am amply supplied.
(Philippians 4:18a NAS)

God, our loving and faithful Father, has promised in His Word to take care of His children—to provide all that we need to fulfill His purposes for our lives. We can trust Him for sufficiency. Provision, of course, is subject to God's definition and measure! We will be given all that is necessary to do the work He has placed before us to do, and with something "extra" that we can give to others.

Help Your beloved servant to trust You today, O Lord, to provide all that she needs—with an overflow amount that she might give to others in need.

> O Lord, heavenly Father, in whom is the
> fullness of light and wisdom, enlighten our
> minds by your Holy Spirit, and give us
> grace to receive your Word with reverence
> and humility, without which no one can
> understand your truth.
>
> —John Calvin

190

A Good Report

[The apostle Paul wrote:]
We give thanks to God, the Father of our Lord Jesus Christ, praying always for you, since we heard of your faith in Christ Jesus and the love which you have for all the saints.
(Colossians 1:3–4 NAS)

How wonderful it is to hear a "good report" about those you love and with whom you have shared the life of Christ Jesus! Few things are more encouraging. The best news is always that our loved ones are continuing in their trust of God, and are continuing in their love of others in the church. What cause for thanks!

May Your beloved one always produce a "good report" because of his faithfulness in serving You and loving other believers in Christ Jesus. Help him today to bring honor to You in everything he undertakes.

191

Eager Anticipation of the Lord's Return

The Spirit and the bride say, "Come."
(Revelation 22:17 NAS)

The New Testament word for "Come" is also presented as "Maranatha!" (See 1 Corinthians 16:22.) This is an Aramaic or Syriac expression that literally means, "our Lord cometh." The statement is not one related to a future coming, but rather, a coming in the present tense! We must be eager for the Lord to return NOW, and to be watching for the next sign of His appearing in our midst. The

Lord will come in that great event we call the Second Coming, but between that moment and this present moment of today, we are to anticipate the Next Coming of the Lord, which could be at any minute. Look for God at work!

Quicken the heart and enlighten the eyes and ears of Your servant, O Lord, to be aware of Your immediate presence and Your "today" work in the NOW of her life.

192

The Quick Sale of Any Items that Needs to Be Sold

She makes linen garments and sells them,
And supplies belts to the tradesmen.
(Proverbs 31:24 NAS)

Many people today are "sellers" of goods and services—sometimes to those in the neighborhood, sometimes to those in faraway places. The internet, the garage sale, and the busy-intersection parking lot have become modern day shopping bazaars! Many people *need* to sell in order to buy necessary food, medicine, and to make payments for shelter and clothing. God not only sees our need, but He has already made provision for that need to be met. We must ask Him to reveal to us where and when we are to access what He desires to give us, and be willing to do the work of "producing and selling" when that is His plan.

Assure Your servant today that You have already prepared all that she needs in order to do all that You are asking of her.

> May Christ be with us! May Christ be before us! May Christ be in us, Christ be over all!
>
> —attributed to St. Patrick

193

Sound Investments

She considers a field and buys it;
From her earnings she plants a vineyard.
(Proverb 31:16 NAS)

God is not opposed to long-term investments, and certainly not to those investments that can yield a short-term harvest! Trust God to lead you to the right investments for you and your family. This passage in the book of Proverbs also states: "She senses that her gain is good." (Proverbs 31:18 NAS) Ask the Lord to impart to you a good sense of what is truly profitable, and what might be a waste of time or money.

You are the Supreme Financial Manager and Investments Adviser, O Lord. Impart wise money-related wisdom to Your child today!

194

Steady Effort

We hear that some among you are leading an undisciplined life, doing no work at all, but acting like busybodies. Now such persons we command and exhort in the Lord Jesus Christ to work in quiet fashion and eat their own bread.
(2 Thessalonians 3:11–12 NAS)

A number of new Christian believers in Thessalonika were so sure that Jesus was coming any second that they quit their jobs and were waiting in slovenly laziness for His arrival. They expected, of course, others who *were* working to feed them at day's end when it was apparent that Jesus was not returning *that* day. While we certainly must be intent and steadfast in our expectation of the Lord's coming, the Lord never admonished His followers to lead undisciplined lives. He expects us to be working when He arrives—eagerly helping others with the fruit of our *labor*. He expects us to be telling others about Him, not engaged in gossip or speculation.

Help Your beloved servant today, O Lord, to lead a disciplined life of work and witness—refraining from idleness and idle talk.

195

Accepting and Heeding God's Chastening

THOSE WHOM THE LORD LOVES HE DISCIPLINES . . . It is for discipline that you endure; God deals with you as with sons; for what son is there whom his father does not discipline.
(Hebrews 12:6–7 NAS)

God does not *punish* His people. God punishes His enemies in order to deliver His people! What God does do is *chasten* His people—all with the intent of guiding them back to the Truth, or instilling in them a new understanding of His righteousness and purposes. Chastening is a process that results in the turning of a person from their will and their self-satisfaction, to God's will and a longing for His approval. Chastening is always for the eternal benefit of the believer—any pain involved is temporary and within the bounds of God's mercy. As the time grows shorter for each of us—either to the day of the Lord's returning or the day of our going to Heaven—we must recognize that our discipline must become *stronger* and our focus *sharper*. We have less and less time, but greater and greater ability, to do more and more!

Help Your child to understand that God wants us *increasingly* to lead disciplined lives that are focused solely on accomplishing His plans and purposes in our lives. Give her a desire to learn quickly the lessons You are teaching!

196

Discerning False Teachers and False Prophets

[Jesus taught:]
"Beware of false prophets, who come to you in sheep's clothing, but inwardly they are ravenous wolves. You will know them by their fruits." (Matthew 7:15–16 NKJV)

The sign of a true prophet is two-fold: First, he gives God's Word to the people without any hesitation or calculation of what will be pleasing to the people. Second, if the prophecy includes a negative consequence or punishment for sin, the true prophet will pray that God has mercy! False prophets usually are intent on telling people what they believe the people WANT to hear, and they rarely care enough about those to whom they prophesy to pray that God will have mercy.

O Lord, bring to light all information that is necessary. Dispel all murkiness and lack of focus. If facts are hidden that need to be revealed, shine Your light of truth on them! If information is purposefully being manipulated or distorted, move in with Your power to destroy all forces of evil and to produce Your accurate understanding. Impart Your wisdom in massive amounts, and reveal anew to Your beloved child that You *always* stand ready to give Your wisdom generously and without any condemnation.

> Persevering prayer produces
> prevailing power.
>
> —Unknown

197

A Crown of Righteousness Laid Up in Glory

There is laid up for me the crown of righteousness, which the Lord, the righteous Judge, will give me on that Day, and not to me only but to all who have loved His appearing
2 Timothy 4:8 NKJV)

Eagerly and intentionally looking for the return of Jesus to this earth is "right" before the Lord. It is a matter of righteousness—being in right standing with God—to desire His immediate presence, and to anticipate His "coming," both in the midst of today's need, and also His Second Coming. Look for Him! Desire Him! Anticipate the "reward" that arrives when He does!

O Lord, help Your child to have an eager anticipation for Your immediate presence, made known as You "arrive" on today's scene, but also arrive in glory in the clouds. Give her an enthusiasm for Your "coming again."

198

Keen Insight into God's Timing and Purposes

We, when we were children, were in bondage under the elements of the world. But when the fullness of the time had come, God sent forth His Son.
(Galatians 4:3–4 NKJV)

The good news for us today in this "historical insight" from the apostle Paul is that God had a precise time for Jesus to be born, not only in history, but to be birthed as "Savior" in each of our lives. Until that moment when we accepted Jesus and were born again, we were truly under bondage to the elements of the world—our culture, our national political structure, and our family limitations. God had a time for freeing us to serve Him, rather than serve mankind. When we are children, we expect to be served—indeed, we expect the entire universe to revolve around us. When we are truly grown up spiritually, we seek only to serve.

Help Your child to be aware of Your timing in his life—to be mindful of the ways in which You have worked to bring about newness of life spiritually, as well as mindful of the responsibilities and privileges he now has as an "adult believer" in service to You.

199

Words of Wisdom

The manifestation of the Spirit is given to each one for the profit of all: for to one is given the word of wisdom through the Spirit.... One and the same Spirit works all these things, distributing to each one individually as He wills.
(1 Corinthians 12:7–8, 11 NKJV)

At all times we are to desire to speak words of wisdom and to trust the Holy Spirit to impart them to us. Wisdom is knowing *how* God desires to see His truth applied in any given situation, relationship, or circumstance. There is never an hour of any day that we are to be "ungifted" in wisdom! The apostle Paul also spoke of the function of this gift, and others, within the context of a church gathering. The Spirit may impart a word of wisdom *through* a believer for the benefit of all believers present. Expect God to use you to speak words of wisdom in your daily life, and to yourself. Be open to His using You to speak to His people in a setting of corporate praise, worship, and Bible teaching.

Impart to Your child, O Lord, words of wisdom directly prompted by Your Spirit and in keeping with Your Word. Let her grow in wisdom with *You* as her tutor.

200

Words of Knowledge

The manifestation of the Spirit is given to each one for the profit of all: for to one is given the word of wisdom through the Spirit, to another the word of knowledge through the same Spirit.... One and the same Spirit works all these things, distributing to each one individually as He wills.
(1 Corinthians 12:7–8, 11 NKJV)

Knowledge is knowing "what"—as well as when, who, and where. Wisdom, in comparison, involves the *application* of information and the godly methods for that application. At times, the Spirit will reveal to a person specific information that previously has gone spiritually undiscerned or physically unperceived, perhaps even intellectually unlearned, so the person might move forward in life with great effectiveness, efficiency, or productivity. This is true on the individual level, as well as in corporate church worship. There is not an hour in a day when we don't need more of God's revealed insight into our lives—knowledge about Him, about others, about ourselves, and knowledge about how to relate to Him and to others. Ask God for knowledge!

Impart to Your child, O Lord, greater knowledge so that she might be of even greater service to You. Be her Teacher in all things, I pray.

> *Beware of placing the emphasis on what prayer costs us; it cost God everything to make it possible for us to pray.*
>
> —Oswald Chambers

201

Freedom from Greed and Covetousness

[God said through Moses:]
"You shall not covet your neighbor's house; you shall not covet your neighbor's wife or his male servant or his female servant or his ox or his donkey or anything that belongs to your neighbor.
(Exodus 20:17 NAS)

A greedy, grasping spirit—an unending desire to acquire or amass more and more and more—is nearly always rooted in covetousness. We engage in a "competition" with others around us, not only to the extent of keeping up with our neighbors, but keeping up or exceeding virtually everybody we encounter or hear about! And why do we covet? We think that by having MORE, we will be more acceptable not only to our peers but to God. We ultimately are striving to earn our way into God's favor and into eternal life by what we accomplish, possess, or rule over. Check your own desire for acquiring MORE. Very likely you do not NEED more, you only WANT more. Ask yourself "why?" The antidote for greed? Give to a needy person generously of what it is you think you "must have." The antidote for covetousness? Give to your neighbor something you value!

Free your beloved child today from a spirit of greed and covetousness, O Lord. Give her a deep satisfaction with what You have provided for her, and give her a desire to share generously with others.

*Praying is letting one's own heart
become the place where the tears of
God and the tears of God's children can
merge and become tears of hope.*

—Henri Nouwen

202

Freedom from Envy and Jealousy

Envy is rottenness to the bones.
(Proverbs 14:30 NKJV)

Envy is wanting something that another person has, with an unrelenting desire for it. It is wanting something for yourself—possession, recognition, or position—that has been awarded to another. Jealousy, in comparison, is a desire to protect and guard something that is rightfully yours. Thus, God can be "jealous" for His own people—wanting to keep them from the clutches of the enemy. Excessive human jealousy can become cloying or manipulative. Excessive envy can eat a person up with unmet desires. Both, the Scriptures say, set up a deep inner frustration and bitterness that can destroy a person's health—both emotionally and physically!

Help Your child, Heavenly Father, to trust You for all things that YOU regard as beneficial for her, without any regard for what You have given or are giving to others. Help her to guard the relationships that You give to her, and to cherish others without smothering them. Help her to value the things You give to her, without hoarding or exalting them.

203

Assurance of Fullness of Life in Christ

We desire that each one of you show the same diligence to the full assurance of hope until the end, that you do not become sluggish, but imitate those who through faith and patience inherit the promises.
(Hebrews 6:11–12 NKJV)

Biblical hope is always linked to heaven—to eternal life in the glorious presence of God the Father and Jesus the Son. We can become "sluggish" in our hope when we begin to take one of these viewpoints: one, a belief that heaven isn't real, or two, a belief that every person ever born will be there. The New Testament tells us otherwise—Jesus spoke of Heaven as a real place with a real system of protocol; He also made it clear that everlasting life belongs only to those who willfully and intentionally choose to accept God's gracious mercy and forgiveness of sin. The writer of Hebrews called upon first-century believers to a life of faith and patience—always anticipating Heaven, but always accepting that our arrival there will be at God's timing. Until that moment, we live in anticipation of Heaven by abiding by Heaven's rules ("thy kingdom come, thy will be done on earth") and trusting God to help us live both as strangers and Christ's ambassadors on this earth.

I trust You today, heavenly Father, to help Your beloved child to remain diligent in her hopes related to eternal life and eternal reward. Help her to exercise active faith and renewed patience as You reveal, and then work out, Your plan and purposes in her life.

204

Refusing to Engage in Worldly and Empty Chatter

Shun profane and idle babblings, for they will increase to more ungodliness. And their message will spread like cancer.
(2 Timothy 2:16–17 NKJV)

"Profane" speech dishonors God. "Idle" speech is speculative, self-promoting (some Bible versions use the word "vain" for "idle"), and unproductive (often in the form of gossip, criticism, or judgment). We are to turn from both profane and idle speech, and we definitely are not to "babble on" in ways that dishonor God or fail to promote the highest and best Christ-like behavior in ourselves or others. Such speech not only leads to ungodly *behavior*, but it always infects those who hear it. It plants ungodly thoughts in the minds of the hearers, and also results in a "did you hear?" frame of mind that leads others to pass on gossip, speculation, criticism, or judgment. Keep in mind that Paul was writing to his colleague in ministry—there is *especially* no benefit in a church leader "telling tales" or using speech that dishonors God. The effects are multiplied, and never justified.

Help Your beloved child today, O Lord, to speak always in a way that honors You and builds up others in Christ.

205

A Keen Awareness of God's Abiding Presence

[Jesus said:]
"Abide in Me, and I in you. As the branch cannot bear fruit of itself, unless it abides in the vine, neither can you, unless you abide in Me." (John 15:4 NKJV)

To abide is to "reside without changing residence." It is a word that applies to all things positional—in other words, "place." We abide in relationships that are rooted in vows before God, or in our commitments to others. We especially abide in our relationship with Christ Jesus. We abide in believing God's Word. We abide in fellowship with other believers (staying planted in the church body where God has led us). It is *only* when we abide in Christ that HIS power and presence flow in us and through us freely and effectively. Only those who abide can bear the fruit of God's Spirit.

Give Your child today a deep awareness of the importance of abiding daily in Your presence, O Lord. Flow in her and through her with Your life-giving, fruit-bearing power.

206

Meeting the Established Goal and Deadline

[Jesus said:]
"Which of you, intending to build a tower, does not sit down first and count the cost, whether he has enough to finish it—lest, after he has laid the foundation, and is not able to finish, all who see it begin to mock him, saying, 'This man began to build and was not able to finish.'"
(Luke 14:28–30 NKJV)

Every project begins with a dream of some sort, but if that dream is not turned into a goal that is clearly stated, the dream will remain dormant. Every goal must be turned into a PLAN, which includes a set of specific actions aimed at a series of goals on a timeline that has periodic benchmarks as "deadlines." Even our relationships need to be put into the context of a plan for their ongoing renewal and growth! Starting isn't enough. One must pursue and *finish*.

Heavenly Father, give Your beloved one a dream from you. Help her to turn it into a goal and to make a plan for meeting that goal. Give her insight so she might make the right plan, and give her the mental, emtional, and spiritual strength to pursue the plan. Help her today to make progress—to some degree and in some way—toward accomplishing Your plans and purposes for her life.

207

Open and Clear Lines of Communication

Your yes is to be yes, and your no, no, so that you may not fall under judgment.
(James 5:12 NAS)

The best form of communication is the conveying of a message without any static, doubt, innuendo, or subtext. In other words, the best communication is clear, personal, and straightforward! The height of clarity comes when we see life in crisp terms of right and wrong, and then root our communication in saying yes to what is right and no to what is wrong. "Yes" and "no" are complete sentences! Anything added to those answers when it comes to our decision-making can confuse others, and at times, be confusing to our own selves! Confusion is the breeding ground for error.

Give clear insight into what You want Your child to do today, and let her answer be a resounding "yes" to Your leading. Help her to convey her choices and decisions clearly to others, especially to those impacted directly by Your revealed plan.

208

Consistency

He who stands steadfast in his heart, having no necessity, but has power over his own will . . . does well.
(1 Corinthians 7:37 NKJV)

The apostle Paul wrote this in the context of teaching believers that it is acceptable to God both to marry or to remain a lifelong virgin. The final decision doesn't matter as much as knowing God's plan for one's life and living it out. The principle of steadfastness and consistency applies to many other situations in life. We are not to be ruled by our passions, nor are we to act solely to satisfy the wishes of others. Rather, we are to determine in our own hearts what it is that God is requiring of us, and then exercise the power of our own will to obey God with steadfastness, a firm and unwavering purpose, loyalty, and resolve that becomes a "bedrock consistency." Our steadfastness should be something others can *count* on, even as we rely on God to help us stay firmly fixed on His will.

Help Your beloved one today, O Lord, to know what you are requiring of her, and enable her to live out Your will in steadfast resolve. Give her an even consistency in her life that cannot be shaken by inner temptations or outer demands from others.

209

Favor

For You, O LORD, will bless the righteous;
With favor You will surround him as with a shield.
(Psalm 5:12 NKJV)

Favor often refers to preferential treatment. This "special" opportunity or treatment is usually expressed with an approving, supportive, friendly attitude. God promises favor to those who are in right relationship with Him. Other people who may not initially like or admire us, may find that they cannot help but be drawn to us or that they cannot help but respond to us with lovingkindness. That's God's favor!

Surround Your child, Heavenly Father, with favor today. Give her favor with her employer or employees, her clients or patients, her friends and family members, and even the clerks, attendants, and service representatives she encounters in her daily work. Give her full awareness that favor is YOUR work, not something she is earning or deserving.

The most praying souls are the most assured souls.

—Thomas Brooks

210

Insight into God's Desired Methods

Then the LORD spoke to Moses, saying...
"Speak to the rock before their eyes, and it will yield its water; thus you shall bring water for them out of the rock."
(Numbers 20:8 NKJV)

God has a way for us to do every thing He calls us to do. We must never assume that the "old way" we have done something—even under God's direction—is going to be God's new way! Moses, early in his leading the Israelites out of Egypt and toward the Land of Promise, had been led by God to strike a rock. When he obeyed, water gushed out. This time, God told him to SPEAK to the rock. The rock was not unlike the previous rock; the result was the same—an abundance of water. The method was to be different, for different purposes. We must keep in mind always that God's METHODS convey a message, which is often as potent as the accomplishment of the goal toward which the method and message are aimed. HOW we live is a key factor in conveying FOR WHOM we live and with what HOPE we live.

Show your servant, O Lord, when to cooperate, and when to contend or compete. Reveal the best methods to use for the most noble goals. Help Your beloved child to see that not all opposition is a call to battle, and that not all alliances are ones that are rooted in a shared understanding of truth or in a shared pursuit of a common goal. Give Your child insight about *how* to contend for the faith, and how to stand firm in righteousness, without bringing undue harm to important relationships.

Prayer is conversation with God.

—*Clement of Alexandria*

211

Sufficient Income

God shall supply all your need according to His riches in glory by Christ Jesus.
(Philippians 4:19 NKJV)

God never promises to give us everything we WANT, but He does promise to supply all we NEED. The "riches" in glory are without limitation—there is no shortage in Heaven. The giver of riches is Christ Jesus, who gives what He knows will further our purpose on this earth and bring us genuine delight. What God authorizes, God funds.

Help Your child, Heavenly Father, to trust You to give him all that is necessary for him to fulfill Your purpose for him on this earth.

212

Growing in Faith

We are bound to thank God always for you, brethren, as it is fitting because your faith grows exceedingly.
(2 Thessalonians 1:3 NKJV)

The Bible makes it clear that each person is given a measure of faith with which to believe that God exists and that God desires a relationship with mankind. (See Romans 12:3 and Romans 1.) That is our starting point in faith, but it is not intended to be our ending point! We are to grow in our faith. How so? By obediently undertaking the challenges God places in our path, trusting God for His help and guidance. The more we put God to the "test," the more He proves Himself trustworthy, and the quicker we are to exercise faith in the future. Our spiritual growth has no "finish line" during our earthy lifetime!

I ask You today, O Lord, to call Your child to greater tests of trust in You, so she might grow in her faith.

213

Extending Hospitality

Be hospitable to one another without complaint.
(1 Peter 4:9 NAS)

Warm fellowship should flow freely among believers. Nothing should be withheld from a believer in need if it is within the capacity of another to meet that need. It was in this way that the first-century Christians in Jerusalem were able to survive after their families and colleagues shunned them for expressing faith in Christ Jesus. Hospitality extended to fellow Christians is still one of the most profound means of witnessing about God's love and saving mercy to unbelievers, and one of the greatest forms of comfort to other Christians

Give Your beloved servant opportunities to extend hospitality, with warmth and generosity. Let her home be a safe haven filled with Christ's peace, hope, and love.

> *Prayer is not only "the practice of the presence of God," it is the realization of His presence.*
>
> —Joseph Fort Newton

214

Maintaining One's Home as a Safe Haven from Evil

When you lie down, you will not be afraid.
(Proverbs 3:24 NAS)

God is ultimately our "safe haven" from evil, but He also desires that we live together with our families in safe zones—our "homes"—that are filled with His presence, provision, and the joy of salvation. We feel safe when we are free from *fear*. Do your utmost today to encourage yourself and others in your family to trust God for all that you need, including a freedom from worry, anxiety, and fear. Encourage one another to believe that God is the Source of all you need, and that He is your loving Provider. Take a family-wide "home audit" and remove from your home anything that detracts from the purity and lovingkindness of Christ Jesus. Ask yourselves, "Is there anything that we would be reluctant to show or share with Jesus if He showed up on our doorstep?" If so, toss it.

Impart to Your child today, O Heavenly Father, a deep sense of security in You—that she can rest in her own home free of evil influences and oppression.

215

Recognizing Truth from Lie

[Jesus said:]
"You will know the truth and the truth will make you free."
(John 8:32 NAS)

God may not impart to us the "information" we think we need or desire, but He always imparts to us the TRUTH that is essential for our eternal destiny and our earthly benefit. That truth is manifested in His Word—the Bible, in Christ Jesus, and in the counsel of the Holy Spirit, the Spirit of Truth. To know life's "answers," we must know the Lord, the giver of life. The more intimate a person's relationship with the Lord, the easier it is for that person to discern the lies that are fired at him by the enemy of his soul.

Help Your child to know the truth and to walk in confident boldness that he is making the right choices and decisions, and manifesting the right behaviors in keeping with Your will.

216

Using Spiritual Gifts to Benefit Others

For to each one is given the manifestation of the Spirit for the common good.
(1 Corinthians 12:7 NAS)

Know your spiritual gifts! You have been given one or more gifts to serve Christ in His church. (See Romans 12.) You are also to be willing to manifest any of the gifts of the Holy Spirit as the Spirit wills. (See 1 Corinthians 12.) Do not be afraid to use your gifts—they are intended to be a blessing to others and God will ensure that they ARE a blessing if they are manifested with love.

Give your child an opportunity to use her spiritual gifts today to bless another believer. Give her boldness in sharing Your love.

Seek help, but even more, seek God.

—Anonymous

217

Judging One's Own Self Rightly

If we judged ourselves rightly, we would not be judged.
(1 Corinthians 11:31 NAS)

It is better to evaluate one's self and make necessary mid-course corrections than to face criticism from others for things you know should have addressed! This verse, of course, does not mean that any person will slide through life criticism-free. Believers in Christ Jesus will always encounter others who *will* criticize, judge, and even condemn them for no reason OTHER than their faith in the Lord. No person should expect a criticism-free life.

Help Your beloved child, O Lord, to face up to the things that You desire to see changed in her life. Assure her of Your help in changing ungodly habits into godly ones. Help her to ignore the criticisms of others that are unwarranted or are rooted in a rejection of Christ Jesus.

218

Owning Up to Sin

I know my transgressions,
And my sin is ever before me.
(Psalm 51:3 NAS)

Before a person can truly be at peace on the inside, he must be free from guilt. And before a person can be free of guilt, he must be forgiven for the sins that create a sense of guilt. And before a person can be forgiven, he must confess his sins before God and ask for God's forgiveness. And before a person confesses his sin, he must own up to the fact that he has sinned and is responsible for his sins. We must never run from our sins. We can't hide from them—or from God. We each must face our sins and take them to God with humble sorrow, and be set free from them through His outpouring of forgiveness. The sequence for dealing with guilt is always: face the reality of sin, confess it to God, be forgiven by God, and then forgive one's self.

Help Your child to own up to his sins, O Lord. Convict him by the power of your Holy Spirit so he will have a full awareness of what is causing the restlessness and guilt in his soul. As he comes to you in humble confession, forgive him, O Lord!

219

Transparency before the Lord

Search me, O God, and know my heart:
Try me, and know my anxieties.
And see if there is any wicked way in me,
And lead me in the way everlasting
(Psalm 139:23–24 NKJV)

Anxieties are those frustrations and worries that nag at us, and that are evidence of a lack of "trust" in the Lord. When we are filled with anxiety, we usually seek to pursue our own answers and solutions to life's problems—we seek our own way, rather than trust God to act in His ways, in His timing, and for His purposes. We are wise to ask God to show us the areas of our life in which we are *not* trusting Him completely, and then to confess this lack of trust and ask for His help.

Help Your child, O Lord, to trust You in all things. Show her that the areas of her "worry" are the areas in which she is not trusting You completely. Give her a desire to trust You more.

220

Deeply Meaningful Communion with the Lord

My eyes are continually toward the LORD.
(Psalm 25:15 NAS)

Communion is not a matter of communication alone, nor is it limited to partaking of the elements of bread and wine as part of the Eucharistic Feast. Communion is spiritual intimacy—a feeling of shared identity and fellowship with God and with other believers. Communion is not a event, but rather, a state of being. Communion with the Lord is not only a matter of quality time, but also "quantity" of time. Those who are in deep communion with our Heavenly Father are those who see Him in every act and experience of life, and who see Him represented by every created thing and person. An all-the-time awareness of the Lord enables a person to hear the Lord's voice, and to feel the Lord's presence, "in the moment" and therefore, "always."

Draw Your beloved servant, O Lord, into deep communion with You.

221

Confidence without Arrogance

Though a host encamp against me,
My heart will not fear;
Though war arise against me,
In spite of this I shall be confident.
(Psalm 27:3 NAS)

No person is totally confident in himself—such a person is more likely arrogant, which is an attitude of self- importance that has *no* regard for others, often to the point of contempt for others. Confidence is rooted in relationship with God. The person who has a personal relationship with Almighty God is the person who should manifest a confident belief that God has promised to be on the side of His beloved children at all times and in all situations. Nothing more is necessary for a person to act boldly and as the Spirit leads!

Give Your child, Father, a strong awareness that You are her protector and provider at all times. Give her confidence in her relationship with You, and enable her to fight for righteousness with boldness.

222

A Zeal for Doing the Right Thing

For the sorrow that is according to the will of God produces a repentance without regret, leading to salvation.... For behold what earnestness this very thing, this godly sorrow, has produced in you: what vindication of yourselves, what indignation, what fear, what longing, what zeal, what avenging of wrong!
(2 Corinthians 7:10–11 NAS)

When a believer confronts sin in his or her life, the response should be godly sorrow, and then, a sincere confession and an ongoing reliance upon the Holy Spirit to live in righteousness. The person who seeks to "get right with God" is a person who must trade in self-justification for Christ's true justification and realignment with God the Father. We *should* become indignant with ourselves for our sin, stand in awe at God's mercy, long for full reconciliation with Him, be zealous to live a renewed life, and be eager to make amends with those we have wounded, even as we resist the temptations of the enemy.

Father, give Your beloved servant an acute awareness of the sins that You desire to be confessed, forgiven, and put away. Help your beloved one to embrace Your process of godly sorrow that results in a renewed life.

223

Rescue from Every Work of Evil

The Lord will rescue me from every evil deed, and will bring me safely to His heavenly kingdom; to Him be the glory forever and ever. Amen.
(2 Timothy 4:18 NAS)

Every believer in Christ Jesus can have a strong hope that the Lord will defeat the enemy of their soul, no matter what the devil might throw at him or the obstacles the devil might put in his path. God's promise is that He will bring us safely to Him in heaven, where we will live in His glorious presence for all eternity. The apostle Paul made this statement to his ministry colleague, Timothy, with tremendous *expectation* found in the word "Amen," which means SO BE IT. The Lord *will* do it!

Give Your beloved child full assurance today, O Lord God, that You will not let anything defeat her salvation—she is eternally secure in her relationship with You!

224

Active Relationships with Others in the Body of Christ

If one member suffers, all the members suffer with it; if one member is honored, all the members rejoice with it.
(1 Corinthians 12:26 NAS)

We are to be in relationship with others to the degree that we know when they are hurting, and when they are being honored! This verse speaks to intense personal communication with fellow believers, and a love for the Body of Christ that includes not only a willingness but a *follow-through* in helping those who are suffering and actively celebrating with those who are rejoicing.

Help Your beloved one today, O Father, to have close ties with those in Your Body. Help him to be a friend of the highest order, quick to accommodate and seek to alleviate the hurts of other believers, and also quick to be envy-free and eager to celebrate their successes.

225

Refusing to Be Crushed by Suffering or Affliction

We are afflicted in every way, but not crushed.
(2 Corinthians 4:8a NAS)

We cannot avoid crushing circumstances and afflictions. We can determine how we will respond to them—we can choose to maintain hope and faith. We can CHOOSE *not* to give in to depression, discouragement, or despair. Even in the face of the most severe persecution or difficulty, we can choose to keep our eyes on Jesus and KNOW that, truly, better days lie ahead for us.

Give Your child comfort today in her suffering, pain, trouble, sorrow, or frustrations. Give her the strength of faith and hope to reject the emotions associated with worry and discouragement.

> Prayer is a direct link to peace of mind and perspective. It reminds us of who we are.
>
> —Benjamin S. Carson, M.D.

226

Refusing to Be in Despair During Times of Perplexity

[We are] perplexed, but not despairing.
(2 Corinthians 4:8b NAS)

People become perplexed when they do not have the answers they need or want—they may not know what, how, when, where, who, or why. If the confusion is intensely frustrating, a person can easily fall into despair. The Christian, however, has two advantages. First, even if he doesn't know the answer, he knows Who does know! The answer can always be found in God's wisdom *if* the answer is one God believes we need to have. Second, even if the answer remains a mystery, the Christian can trust that God's benevolence will produce what is good and right.

Help Your child today, O Lord, to look to You and not the problem. You not only know all answers, You *are* the Answer!

227

Courage for Every Day

"Be strong and courageous! Do not tremble or be dismayed, for the LORD your God is with you wherever you go."
(Joshua 1:9 NAS)

This was the charge God gave to Joshua as he prepared to lead the Israelites into conquest of the Promised Land. It is equally good advice for those who are simply going out to conquer their day! We tremble in fear; we are dismayed when we find ourselves frustrated—perhaps thwarted from the good we seek to do, or tripped up by the bad that others dish out. Both fear and dismay are emotions that are within our will to control. We can CHOOSE to be strong and courageous even in the face of fear and discouragement. Truly the Lord is WITH us always. He is entirely willing to be our source of strength and courage!

Help Your child, Heavenly Father, to trust You today for all the courage and strength he needs in the face of all fears, anxieties, frustrations, and disappointments. Assure Your child of Your "ever-presence."

228

Safe Travel

Uphold my steps in Your paths,
That my footsteps may not slip.
(Psalm 17:5 NKJV)

Every journey has risks, known and unknown. We are wise always to ask God to send His holy angels to guard and guide our steps, no matter our destination, the length of our journey, or its importance. Our desire must be to walk in His ways, to bring glory to His name, and to have our steps ordered by Him at all times.

O Lord, give Your beloved child safe travel today, even if it is just a walk out to her garden and a return trip to her kitchen, or a drive to her office and a return drive home. Let the way be smooth, let her fellow travelers be friendly, and let her accomplishment on the way be all that You have established for her to say and do.

> I have been driven many times to my knees by the overwhelming conviction that I had nowhere else to go.
>
> —Martin Luther

229

Full Restoration

"Then I will make up to you for the years
That the swarming locust has eaten,
The creeping locust, the stripping locust and the gnawing locust,
My great army which I sent among you.
You will have plenty to eat and be satisfied
And praise the name of the LORD your God,
Who has dealt wondrously with you;
Then My people will never be put to shame."
(Joel 2:25–26 NAS)

In broad terms, restoration refers to the repair or the replacement of something broken or lost. It also refers to all that the devil or his agents (both spiritual and human) seek to steal, kill, and destroy. Restoration can also refer to a relationship—generally termed "reconciliation"—and especially to the restoration of relationship with God our heavenly Father.

Lord, I pray today that Your relationship with Your beloved child be restored fully. I pray that everything she has lost or had stolen from her will be restored fully—yes, even to an increased measure. I pray that she will trust You fully to heal or repair all that has been broken. Even as You make her whole, I pray that You will create greater order and wholeness in the environment around her.

> *God looks not . . . at the geometry of your prayers, how long they may be; nor at the arithmetic of your prayers, how many they may be; nor at logic of your prayers, how methodical they may be; but the sincerity of them.*
>
> —Thomas Brooks

230

Guidance in the Paths of Righteousness

[David said about the Lord, His Shepherd:]
He leads me in the paths of righteousness
For His name's sake.
(Psalm 23:3 NKJV)

Righteousness refers to "right standing" with God. God desires that we walk in ways that He ordains for us so we might be in the right position at all times to receive *all* of His rewards. At all times, we must trust the Lord to lead us to destinations that are of His choosing, and ultimately, to the destination of our eternal home with Him. A journey in righteousness brings glory to His name!

O Lord, lead Your beloved one in Your paths of righteousness. Let her walk with You and bring glory to Your name.

231

Release from Bondage

[Jesus said:]
"So if the Son makes you free, you will be free indeed."
(John 8:36 NAS)

Bondage refers to all limitations, prisons, shackles, or anything that holds us back from the full pursuit of God's purposes for us, or anything that keeps us from being made whole in Christ Jesus. Bondage includes emotional bondage, often generated by our habits of codependency or by abuse we have experienced in the past. Jesus came to set us free!

Lord, set Your beloved servant *free*! Release her from all bonds that tie her to the past in a way that limits her future. Release her from all ties to others that are unhealthy or hurtful. Release her from the influence of those who are keeping her from the blessings You desire for her. Take off her what the devil has put on her, put in her what the devil has taken out of her, and bring her to wholeness.

232

Finding Your "Role" in the Body of Christ

For just as we have many members in one body and all the members do not have the same function, so we, who are many, are one body in Christ, and individually members one of another. Since we have gifts that differ according to the grace given to us, each of us is to exercise them accordingly.
(Romans 12:4–6 NAS)

Every believer has a role to play in the Body of Christ. This role not only fulfills the believer, but helps all others in the Body. It produces health and wholeness, and is the greatest witness to the unbeliever of God's love and provision to meet *all* manner of need. If you don't know fully what your role is today in the Body of Christ, ask the Lord to show you what He desires for you to do. The role He has for you is one that is perfectly suited to the gifts He has already given you, and will be genuinely helpful to others around you.

Help Your beloved, one, O Lord, to find and fulfill the exact role in Your Body that You have for him. Show Him how to help others, using fully the talents and abilities You have already placed in him. Give him great desire to serve others and bring glory to You.

> I have so much to do today that I shall
> spend the first three hours in prayer.
>
> —Martin Luther

233

God's Anointing

[David said about the Lord, His Shepherd:]
You anoint my head with oil.
(Psalm 23:5b NKJV)

In the Bible, a spiritual anointing with oil (a spiritual leader pouring oil on the head of a person) was a symbol of the outpouring of the Holy Spirit on that person. In a social setting during Bible times, the *providing* of oil for a guest to use on his hair was a sign of gracious hospitality. In the shepherd's world, oil was used as a cleansing and healing agent for sheep that had been wounded, perhaps after a sheep had fallen onto rocks, been attacked by a predator, or had become tangled in thorny underbrush. All forms of "anointing" were experienced by David, who wrote this psalm. He had been anointed by the prophet Samuel to be the future king of Israel. He certainly felt welcomed by the Lord. And, he knew the Lord's provision in healing him from emotional wounds. God's anointing is for ALL who believe in Christ Jesus. It is an anointing of empowerment by the Holy Spirit, an anointing of healing for all facets of life, and an anointing of full welcome in God's house as a member of God's family.

Allow Your servant to experience a fresh "anointing" from You today, O Lord.

234

Deliverance from Distress

The troubles of my heart have enlarged;
Bring me out of my distresses!
(Psalm 25:17 NKJV)

Distress is nearly always linked to mental suffering—deep grief, anxiety, or anticipated happiness denied. Mental and emotional distress increasingly are being linked to physical pain and discomfort. The great news is that God desires to deliver us from *all* forms of distress so that we might walk freely and boldly through each day, bearing witness to God as our Deliverer and Healer.

Help Your child, O Lord, to turn immediately to You at the first sign of internal or external distress, and to trust You for deliverance and healing!

235

Vindication

Vindicate me, O LORD,
For I have walked in my integrity.
I have also trusted in the LORD;
I shall not slip.
(Psalm 26:1 NKJV)

To vindicate a person is to clear that person of all blame, guilt, suspicion, or doubt. It is the highest form of "defense" and justice. Trust God to "clear your name" today of any false accusations. Refuse to take vengeance into your own hands.

Thank You, Lord, for Your vindicating power. Set Your child free today from all verbal and physical assaults that attempt to diminish his witness or destroy his integrity. Preserve Your good name embodied in Your beloved child.

*The greatest privilege God gives to you is
the freedom to approach Him at any time.*

—Wesley L. Duewel

236

Exuberance in Dancing before the Lord

David was dancing before the LORD with all his might.
(2 Samuel 6:14a NAS)

The type of dancing that David demonstrated was a spontaneous, full-body expression of joy for what the Lord had done, was doing, and had promised to do. It was a dance of exuberant thanks and praise. No choreography. No forethought. No partner other than the Lord Himself. And no music required other than the believer's own spiritual song. To dance before the Lord is an expression of sublime submission and total submission to God's purposes.

Lord, give Your beloved child and opportunity to dance before You today!

237

Guidance from the Lord

[The Lord said through the prophet Isaiah:]
"I am the LORD your God . . .
Who leads you in the way you should go."
(Isaiah 48:17b NAS)

Guidance in the Bible is very often expressed in terms of "leading"—God leads His people as a good Shepherd, to pastures. He gives His people answers, direction, and solutions. But He does so "leading the way," not just pointing out the way. The good news about God's leading is that He is always "out front," scouting the way, destroying the enemies in advance, and setting the path for maximum provision and purpose.

O Lord, help Your child today to trust You to lead her, step by step, along the way You have chosen for her. Prepare the way, and prepare her to walk in it!

238

Refuge in a Time of Attack

You have been a defense for the helpless,
A defense for the needy in his distress,
A refuge from the storm, a shade from the heat.
(Isaiah 25:4 NAS)

Life attacks us in many ways—from people who seek to exert power over us or control of us, to our own inner attacks of fear and anxiety, to the attacks of nature in the form of storms or catastrophes. The prophet Isaiah also pointed out in this same verse, "The breath of the ruthless is like a rain storm against a wall." The attacks of life seek to wear us down, eroding us bit by bit. God provides a shelter from it all—HIMSELF!

O Lord, reveal to Your beloved child today that YOU are his place of refuge. As he spends time in calm meditation before You, pour out Your assurance into his heart that You are his deliverer and mainstay.

*Prayer without watching is hypocrisy;
and watching without prayer is
presumption.*

—William Jay

239

An Outpouring of God's Lovingkindness

[The Lord spoke through the prophet Jeremiah:]
"I have loved you with an everlasting love;
Therefore I have drawn you with lovingkindness."
(Jeremiah 31:3 NAS)

God loves, and in loving us, He extends Himself toward us to draw us toward Himself! His love has purpose—to build relationship with us. The word lovingkindness in Hebrew is *chesed*. It refers to a love that is loyal—in other words, love that fulfills all covenants made by the Lover. God does not withdraw from us—ever. His love is abiding, persistent, and generous, ever merciful and faithful.

Help Your beloved one, O Lord, to recognize and receive the lovingkindness that You seek to pour into her life. Help her to feel Your love drawing her ever closer to You. Give her perspective that You have always loved her, and always will.

240

Recognizing God at Work

Come and see the works of God.
(Psalm 66:5 NKJV)

God is at work in our individual lives, in our "corporate" life as part of both our individual church body and the Church around the world, and in the world at large—at all times and throughout history. God has never disengaged himself from His creative process or His control of all that He has made. We often, however, must *look* diligent for the work of God, *especially* in times, situations, and relationships that seem confused or filled with ongoing difficulty. In those times God's work is not always *obvious*—it is ongoing nonetheless. Ask God to give you a glimpse into His work—including His plans, purposes, and methodologies. Ask Him to show you how YOU fit into the schematic of His whole.

Reveal to Your beloved servant, O Lord, a glimpse today of "God at Work!" Let her begin by looking into the mirror of her own soul. Give her joy in knowing that Your work is ongoing, and that no "God project" is finished until YOU say that it is. Help her to comprehend that all of Your projects end in Your saying, "It is GOOD!"

241

A Soul that Thirsts for the Presence of God

As the deer pants for the water brooks,
So pants my soul for You, O God.
My soul thirsts for God, for the living God.
(Psalm 42:1–2a NKJV)

Two concepts intersect in this verse. First, we and all other living creatures on the earth *must* have water for life. That is true in the natural, and for mankind, it is also true in the spiritual. We must have the refreshing and renewing water of the Holy Spirit flowing in our life daily. This cleansing and renewing flow of the Spirit was first made possible to us in our baptism, which was the outward sign of an inner cleansing. Second, water is scarce in the Bible lands. The ibex that roam the wilderness hills in Israel often come to sources of water after long, hot, dry wandering. The same is true for us. We can sometimes feel "dry" spiritually, but God promises us that if we search for Him—and desire Him deeply as an absolute *essential*— our thirst for the Lord will be satisfied. Remember that Jesus said those who hunger and *thirst* for righteousness shall be satisfied. (See Matthew 5:6.)

Heavenly Father, meet the need of Your child today for true spiritual refreshment and renewal—satisfy her thirst for You!

242

God Making a Way When No Way Seems Possible

[The Lord spoke through the prophet Hosea:]
"I knew you in the wilderness,
In the land of great drought."
(Hosea 13:5 NKJV)

For forty years, the Israelites wandered in a great "wilderness" between their past in Egypt and their future in the Promised Land. God reminded them centuries later of His presence with them, providing the very things that they could not find in the wilderness. He gave them water—even out of a rock. He gave them food—manna daily. He allowed the things they had to "last" and not wear out since there were no shops from which to purchase items. He gave them direction, even in regions with shifting sands. God is entirely capable of providing for us, protecting us, and guiding us even if there are no man-made road signs, rest stops, or paved highways!

Lord, help Your child today to trust You in every difficult and confusing situation to provide ALL that she needs, ALWAYS.

He who runs from God in the morning will scarcely find Him the rest of the day.

—John Bunyan

243

Awareness of the Beauty God Bestows

[Jesus said:]
"Consider the lilies of the field, how they grow; they neither toil nor spin; and yet I say to you that even Solomon in all his glory was not arrayed like one of these."
(Matthew 6:28b–29 NKJV)

God desires that we be aware of beauty, and see the beauty of nature as His provision to us. Natural beauty reminds us of the perfection of the Garden of Eden before the Fall. It reminds us that sin always destroys beauty, even though it may initially promise greater glory. Beauty also reminds us that God will one day restore all things to beautiful perfection—we are to anticipate that day with joy!

Give Your child a deep awareness of beauty all around him today. Let him see this as Your gift, and Your promise. Help him to add to the beauty of his life in practical ways.

244

Wisdom to Make a Right Choice

"I, wisdom, dwell with prudence,
And I find knowledge and discretion.
The fear of the LORD is to hate evil;
Pride and arrogance and the evil way
And the perverted mouth, I hate."
(Proverbs 8:12–13 NAS)

God promises wisdom to any person who asks Him for it! (See James 1:5.) He gives wisdom in generous amounts, without any criticism of us for *not* automatically having wisdom. Wisdom is knowing HOW God perceives things, does things, and desires to do things. Many people start with their limited human knowledge, and then attempt to cobble it together with a worldview in order to have "understanding" so they will know what to do and how to act. God says, "start with Me." If you want to know something, "ask Me." God promises to give us the *why* that is the best foundation for knowing all that is necessary for us to know, and also to know how the pieces of our life fit together.

Lord, help Your beloved child today to seek Your wisdom, and as a consequence of finding it, to have greater knowledge, more discretion, a clearer understanding of right and wrong, a stronger hatred of evil, and an increased desire for humility and association with others who are humble and righteousness. Impart ample wisdom to her for every major choice and decision she faces today.

245

Loving Others as God Loves

This commandment we have from Him: that he who loves God must love his brother also.
(1 John 4:21 NKJV)

God has never made a person He did not love fully, generously, and unconditionally. God is motivated by love—a reaching out to His creation in hopes of full reconciliation with every person who will believe and receive His free offer of forgiveness and mercy. If we are to become more like Jesus, we must love as He loved and serve as He served. No criticism of man must be allowed to muddy the pure flow of love from our hearts.

I do not pray for success. I ask for faithfulness.

—Mother Teresa

Help Your beloved one today, O Lord, to manifest more love toward others. Give her a deep motivation to love as You love—no matter what others do to her or say about her.

246

Loving What God Loves and Hating What God Hates

The fear of the LORD is the beginning of knowledge.
(Proverbs 1:7 NAS)

A basic knowledge of right and wrong is essential. We are born with a conscience waiting to be used, but our inbred conscience needs to be "informed" with a knowledge of good (what God loves) and evil (what God hates). The only place to gain reliable information about good and evil is God's Word. Parents sometimes get it wrong. The same for others in authority positions. Only God, who made the "rules" of right and wrong, and who also gave us our conscience, can impart ACCURATE, universal, abiding, and trustworthy information about what we should pursue and what we should avoid. We must "fear" (which means to have holy awe and respect for) God's position of absolute authority and power. Until we come to that point, we will not truly have an open heart and to receive the knowledge, understanding, and wisdom God desires to give us.

Heavenly Father, help Your beloved one to love what You love, and hate what You hate, and above all, to turn to You any time he has a question about what YOU consider to be right and wrong.

> *We are living in dangerous times and if there was ever a time when we need to pray, it's now.*
>
> —Billy Graham

247

Seeing the Consequences

Your word is a lamp to my feet
And a light to my path.
(Psalm 119:105 NAS)

Think of holding a flashlight on a dark night in the forest. The path is there, but you must be able to see it in order to walk safely on it. When you shine the flashlight (lamp) toward your feet, you see the next step that can be taken securely. When you shine the flashlight down the path, you see the future direction you are to take. God's Word gives us both direction for today's challenges, and also shows us the direction we are to take from today all the way to eternity. God's Word covers both the immediate and the future—it is both timely and eternal.

Reveal to Your beloved servant all that she needs to know about the consequences related to today, and the consequences related to eternity. Give her a sense of what is timely and temporal, and what is intended to be everlasting. Give her both promises and warnings, and help her to make the right choices in every situation she encounters.

248

Enduring Wealth

Riches and honor are with me,
Enduring riches and righteousness.
(Proverbs 8:18 NKJV)

The real "wealth" of a person does not lie in what he or she HAS, but in who they BECOME. Material wealth is for this life only. True inner wealth of character and righteousness are forever. The riches of Christ Jesus—His nature, His presence and power, His provision and protection—are the only forms of wealth that last forever and lead to ongoing purpose and fulfillment throughout eternity.

Give Your child, O Heavenly Father, a deep desire for the "enduring riches" and righteousness that are found in You alone. Turn her eyes from the temporal to the eternal.

249

Living above Reproach

You now my reproach, my shame, and my dishonor . . . .
Reproach has broken my heart . . . .
Let Your salvation, O God, set me on high.
(Psalm 69:19–20, 29 NKJV)

Much of Psalm 69 is about reproach that comes in the wake of the person having been a faithful follower of the Lord. This reproach is tantamount to shame. It is unwarranted and God promises to deliver the faithful person from "feelings" of reproach. A different kind of reproach is sometimes experienced as a direct result of personal sin. The cure for that reproach is confession and the receiving of God's forgiveness. In both cases, God's desire is for His people to live free of reproach. We are to refuse to harbor shame for things we did not do (false guilt) or for giving testimony to the love of God. We are to cast off the reproach related to our sin by seeking and receiving God's forgiveness—and in many cases, by following through on *God's* forgiveness by forgiving ourselves and choosing to move forward in our lives by the grace of God.

Help Your beloved servant, O Lord, to live "above" all accusations of shame that he does not deserve, and if any occasion arises in which he does something warranting contempt or blame, to run to You quickly for forgiveness. Do not let Your child get bogged down in self-recrimination or guilt!

250

Godly Counselors

Where there is no counsel, the people fall;
But in the multitude of counselors there is safety.
(Proverbs 11:14 NKJV)

We each see only a portion of the world, in a limited context and a limited frame of time. We cannot perceive everything, know everything, or gain enough background information on our own to make thoroughly good choices and decisions. We must have God as our supreme Counselor—indeed, Jesus referred to the Holy Spirit as the One who would be our Spirit of Truth. We also must avail ourselves of the insights of wise counselors—those who love God, desire His leading of their lives, and who have a wide background of experience and accurate information. The true purpose of "diversity" is to get multiple sources of information (not to accept all diverse viewpoints as equal or to adopt all viewpoints as one's own).

I pray today, O Lord, that You would put MANY godly counselors into the path of Your beloved child. Let her weigh their advice against the absolute wisdom of Your Word and Your Holy Spirit. Lead her to safety as she makes choices and decisions today.

He who fails to pray does not cheat God. He cheats himself.

—George Failing

251

Having No Idols

[The Lord said through the prophet Ezekiel:]
"Repent and turn away from your idols."
(Ezekiel 14:6a NAS)

Idols in ancient times were carved images intended to represent various "gods." The placing of offerings of food and drink before these gods was a sign of giving homage to the god, in hopes of favors in return, primarily fertility, protection from natural disasters, good crops and healthy livestock, and other means of natural provision. God's desire was that His people look to HIM for all protection and provision, that they serve Him in their hearts and in their deeds, and that they regard Him as the one and true Source of all things, including their very lives. God's plan is no different today. He wants us to place our total trust in Him, not in the systems of this world, the government, financial institutions or investment portfolios, or in any other man-made or man-generated means or methods of protection and supply.

Help Your child, O Lord, to trust You fully—for all things. Give her an insight that You and You alone are her Source of all good supply. Give her an understanding that there is no "work of her hands" that will produce what Your presence produces in her and through her.

> Between the humble and contrite heart
> and the majesty of heaven there are no
> barriers; the only password is prayer.
>
> —Montaigne

252

Turning Away from All Abominations

[The Lord said through the prophet Jeremiah:]
"Return to Me;
And if you will put away your abominations out of My sight,
Then you shall not be moved."
(Jeremiah 4:1 NKJV)

An abomination is a behavior or object that God detests to the point that He would utterly wipe it out if He had not given mankind free will to choose abominations. Many deeds declared to be abominations come with a death sentence in the Old Testament. God hates evil and one day will utterly wipe out all evil. Until that day, He calls us to denounce and cease from all things He calls abominations, and to draw close to Him. Only then can we be assured of His protection and provision for us in the face of an evil generation.

Help Your child today, O Lord, to turn from everything that You have clearly stated You detest and will one day destroy. Help her to choose YOU over any other person. Help her to pursue what YOU declare to be good and right, even if all others are trying to convince her otherwise. Keep her steady and steadfast as she takes a stand for godliness.

253

A Listening Heart

Listen, O my people, to my instruction;
Incline your ears to the words of my mouth.
I will open my mouth in a parable;
I will utter dark sayings of old,
Which we have heard and known,

And our fathers have told us.
(Psalm 78:1-2 NAS)

Every conversation we have has a nugget of instruction in it—we can and must learn from others, either things to do or things NOT to do. To learn from others you must listen intently—this means listening to what is NOT being said as much as to what IS being said. Ask the Lord to show you what is being said that bears witness to His truth, and to reveal what is being said that supports the enemy's lies against you. Listen not only with your ears, but with your spirit.

Help Your beloved one, O Lord, to hear YOU speaking through the mouths of godly people, and also to hear YOU speak in her spirit giving warning when ungodly people seem persuasive. Incline her heart toward You, and then as Your child, incline her heart to those who can give her sound instruction for living a godly life in today's world.

254

Healed Wounds

[Jesus] touched his ear and healed him.
(Luke 22:51 NAS)

In the Garden of Gethsemane, at the time of Jesus' arrest, one of Jesus' disciples used a sword to slash at one of the members of the arresting party, and in so doing, he sliced off the man's outer ear. Jesus, in the midst of the confusion and terror of the moment, took time to restore this man's ear, healing him instantly. Wounds are nearly always inflicted from others, or from life's circumstances. We don't need to have enemies to be wounded. Random accidents happen, and total strangers can wound us unintentionally or intentionally. God makes it clear, however, that He is never too busy to stop and heal our wounds. We must ask Him to heal not only for our physical wounds, but our inner emotional, mental, and spiritual wounds.

Heal Your beloved child today, O Father. Bring her relief from pain, stop any forces of infection, and renew her spirit, mind, and body.

255

Self-Restraint

[The Lord said through the prophet Ezekiel:]
"Turn your faces away from all your abominations."
(Ezekiel 14:6b NAS)

God calls us to use our gift of free will to make wise choices about life. He calls us to godly self-management! The life that is truly "under godly control" is a life that is in total obedience to God's law *without ever having to give thought to God's law!* The godly person led by the Spirit will automatically *do and say* what is righteous according to God's Word. We are wise to ask the Holy Spirit to impart to us a willingness to restrain our own impulses, and to seek to make intentional wise choices that are in line with God's plans and purposes. Self-management is proactive and positive. Those who engage in godly self-management avoid, rather than fight, temptation whenever possible.

Help Your beloved one, O Lord, to exercise sound self restraint, and in so doing, to pursue in a proactive way all that You desire for her. Show her that the key to self-management is allowing YOU to have greater input and leadership of her life.

When we serve the Lord with our whole heart, we have confidence and joy in prayer.

—Unknown

256

Protection in a Time of Catastrophe

The LORD shall preserve you from all evil;
He shall preserve your soul.
(Psalm 121:7 NKJV)

God does not promise to spare us from all attacks of evil. He does not promise to remove all consequences of evil. He does promise to *preserve* us from evil, which means that evil will have no lasting or eternal consequences. Our mind and emotions can be shielded from permanent damage. Nothing of evil can touch our eternal relationship with the Lord. Even in times when we feel as if we are in danger of losing everything, or we have lost everything in the material and natural world, we have not lost Christ! His presence with us is abiding, and is the best preservative ever!

Protect and preserve Your servant today, O Lord. Help her to keep her eyes on Your lasting presence, rather than on her temporary circumstances or troubles.

257

Discretion

Discretion will preserve you.
(Proverbs 2:11a NKJV)

Discretion is the exercise of good judgment and sensitivity that keeps others from being embarrassed or unnecessarily upset. It includes the ability to keep a secret and to keep information confidential. There are some things that simply do not *need* to be told—either for the benefit of a person under attack or for the benefit of others in association with that person. If confrontation is necessary, it should be a direct and private confrontation with the offender. Those who are "discreet" keep their own reputation from being sullied by another's sins. Discretion is an act of faith that God can and will deal directly with all who err or sin.

I pray today that You will help Your servant to be discreet—to keep confidential information in confidence, and to protect the secrets of others while YOU do Your work in their lives.

258

A Soft Answer to Combat Anger or Rancor

A gentle answer turns away wrath.
(Proverbs 15:1a NAS)

Two things nearly always escalate or expand anger: volume and rapidly fired statements. If a person sees anger beginning to fester to the point of near eruption in another person, the wisest thing to do to turn down the volume of communication, and to slow the pace of it. Let the angry person know that you would like to discuss the situation, and if a cooling off period is necessary, schedule that discussion for a later time. Don't let negative comments turn into a shouting match that can easily result in things being said in too much haste, without true intention or reason.

I ask You today, dear Father, to help Your beloved child to deal with the angry words of others in a gentle way that diffuses the emotional heat and allows calm solutions to emerge.

259

Refusing to Be Co-Dependent

For each one will bear his own load.
(Galatians 6:5 NAS)

Just a few verses before this one, the apostle Paul calls upon the Galatians to bear one another's burdens. The word "bear" in these verses refers to two very different Greek words. In Galatians 6:2 we are to help bear the burdens of others as part of a collective and short-term effort. It is like a group of people coming together to help lift a heavy boulder off a person after a landslide, thus enabling the person to regain health and strength and then to take up their own load and walk their own path. In Galatians 6:5, the reference is to a person bearing their own personal load of life's work, struggle, and challenge. It is tantamount to letting a person carry their own backpack of small rocks. We are never wise to do for others what they can do for themselves. Nor are we wise to allow others to coerce or manipulate us into being what *they* want us to be *for them*, rather than what *God* wants us to be *for Him*. God desires for us to care for others and to help those in need, but never to the point that we replace Him in their lives—no, not to any degree. We each must learn to trust God for ourselves.

Thank You, Father, for freeing Your beloved child from co-dependency with another person. Help her to be fully dependent upon YOU as her source, her comfort, her guide, and her eternal friend.

> As artists give themselves to their models,
> and poets to their classical pursuits, so
> must we addict ourselves to prayer.
>
> —Charles Spurgeon

260

Kept Vows

When you make a vow to God, do not delay to pay it;
For He has no pleasure in fools.
Pay what you have vowed—
Better not to vow than to vow and not pay.
(Ecclesiastes 5:4–5 NKJV)

Vows are expressions of human will, made out of the "freedom" of human will God has granted to mankind. They are not statements of intent, but rather, statements of firm commitment. In a spiritual court of law, they stand as evidence and are subject to full payment. God does not ask us to "vow," and we are better off not to make a vow than to make one lightly or without full research into all that is required for payment of the vow. Broken vows are a sign of a person's foolishness and spiritual immaturity.

Help Your child today, O Lord, only to voice statements of commitment to You and to others that she can and will keep.

261

Gaining Traction for Forward Motion

As you therefore have received Christ Jesus the Lord, so walk in Him, rooted and built up in Him and established in the faith, as you have been taught, abounding in it with thanksgiving.
(Colossians 2:6–7 NKJV)

Those who find themselves "stuck," seemingly unable to move forward in their lives, likely do not need a "solution" to motivate them, but rather, more of Jesus Christ. They need more of the Holy

Spirit's impartation of who Jesus was, what Jesus accomplished on their behalf, and how Jesus empowers us today through His Spirit. When a person is built up in Christ, and established in faith, it becomes much easier to "walk forward!" The confidence is that *anything* the believer does is going to be better and work out to greater eternal advantage than *anything* the devil does. As in all situations, we are to walk "abounding with thanksgiving." Why? Because of what God has done, is doing, and has promised to do—knowing deep within that what He has promised to do, He *will* do! We cannot fail because He will not fail.

O Lord, help Your child to move forward today toward all that You have planned and purposed for him.

262

Increased Momentum

We are bound to thank God always for you, brethren, as it is fitting, because your faith grows exceedingly, and the love of every one of you all abounds toward each other.
(2 Thessalonians 1:3 NKJV)

What an amazing thing to be known for a faith that is growing *exceedingly*! What an awesome thing to have a reputation for *abounding* love! The Christian life is to be lived with superlatives. "Exceedingly" means "to a very high—unusually high—degree." "Abound" refers to a large quantity, number, or amount. These words are not just end statements or goals. They are process words. We grow from faith to greater faith, from love to greater love. The daily increase is what produces a superlative satisfaction and fulfillment that life is *progressing* as God intends.

Help Your child, dear Father, to grow a little greater in love and faith *today*.

263

Winning the Crown of Life

Blessed is the man who endures temptation; for when he has been approved, he will receive the crown of life which the Lord has promised to those who love him.
(James 1:12 NKJV)

The key to winning is saying "no" to the devil's temptations—which always result in a detour, a delay, or discouragement that paralyzes. We must endure temptations; they will come whether we like them or not. But we do not need to entertain them as fantasies, promote them in our conversations, or engage behaviorally in them. Our "approval" is based upon our saying "no" and trusting God for His "yes" alternatives. The crown of life is not only for eternity, it is a crown that is already ours to wear—it is the crown that Jesus won on our behalf, but it is only worn by us when we are acting as a joint-heir and therefore, a "prince" of the Lord on this earth.

Heavenly Father, I ask You today to help Your beloved child endure and resist all temptations so she might be approved as one worthy to wear a royal crown before others.

264

Righteous Lips

Righteous lips are the delight of kings,
And they love him who speaks what is right.
(Proverbs 16:13 NKJV)

Those who are in authority over people groups nearly always love to listen to those who will speak the truth of God to them! We must not be afraid to voice our beliefs in the Lord Jesus at every opportunity. The leader may not agree with us after listening to us, but the God-appointed rulers over us nearly always will value the courage of our convictions and the insights we convey. Even ungodly rulers have been known to seek out godly citizens to give them godly counsel. Every person wants to succeed—and every person wants to know how to have God on his side to help him succeed. The starting point for a conversation about God may be this statement: "I know God Almighty has put you into the position you hold today."

Gracious Lord, give Your child boldness today to speak truth.

265

Being Given an Opportunity

I rejoiced in the Lord greatly, that now at last you have revived your concern for me; indeed, you were concerned before, but you lacked opportunity.
(Philippians 4:10 NAS)

An opportunity is a "chance"—often one resulting in an advantage, and often as the result of a convergence of favorable circumstances or situations. Who is in control of ALL circumstances? God! There are no *coincidences*, only *God incidents*. When God sends an opportunity, it is an opportunity to do *good*—and that ultimately mean to give of one's time, talent, or resources to serve others in need. The apostle Paul lamented that the Philippians had "lacked opportunity," but now rejoiced that they HAD opportunity and had acted on it. When opportunity arises to do good—ACT ON IT!

Help Your beloved one, O Lord, to be aware of ALL the opportunities You send, and to become diligent in using those moments of advantage and favor for doing good. Bless Your child for capitalizing on opportunities to bless others!

266

A Break

[Naomi said:]
The LORD grant that you may find rest.
(Ruth 1:9a NKJV)

All people need times of relief or respite from their work, including the work associated with the routine chores and responsibilities of life. We can give ourselves a "break" for physical rest, and we can take mini-vacations in our minds to give ourselves mental rest. It is even more important, however, to give ourselves rest emotionally and spiritually. Emotional and spiritual exhaustion are possible, and both can be avoided. How? By simply carving out time to spend in the quiet presence of the Lord, not talking, but listening. Be open to *anything* the Lord may impart to you. It will be for your good, and it will give rest to your weary heart and your restless spirit.

Loving Lord, impart Your rest to Your servant today.

267

Clarity in Decision Making

Then He [Jesus] put His hands on his eyes again and made him look up. And he was restored and saw everything clearly.
(Mark 8:25 NKJV)

God does not desire that His people live in confusion, or in doubt. He wants us to see the TRUTH clearly, and to make sound choices and decisions based on it. God is not the author of confusion—He reveals readily all that we *need* to know to serve Him and fulfill His purposes for our lives. There may be things He does *not* reveal, but in all areas where we must have His wisdom, He imparts it generously, if we only ask in faith for it. (See James 1:5.) We are to ask until we *know* the right thing to do, in the right timing, using the right methods, and for the right reasons. Until we know, we must continue to ask!

Let Your servant see clearly all that is involved so that she can make the decision You desire for her to make, O Lord.

268

Good and Accurate Memory

I will remember the works of the LORD;
Surely I will remember Your wonders of old.
(Psalm 77:11 NKJV)

Memory loss is not God's design! We are to do our utmost to keep our minds active, fully engaged in the pursuit of understanding and wisdom. We are to commit God's Word to memory, and recite it often to ourselves. The quality of what we remember is directly related to the quality of what we encounter, what we ponder, and the experiences we pursue. The best memories are those that are evidence to us of God's tremendous power, provision, protection, and presence with us.

Help Your beloved child, O Lord, to *make* good memories, and to enjoy recalling them. Give her remembrance of the many ways in which You have been with her always, working things to her good now and forever.

269

Valor

The man Jeroboam was a mighty man of valor; and Solomon, seeing that the young man was industrious, made him the officer over all the labor force of the house of Joseph.
(1 Kings 11:28 NKJV)

"Valor" is a word usually reserved for great displays of courage, especially as shown in a battle or war. The word "mighty" at the time of Israel's first kings was a word used to describe people with extreme strength or power. In the case of Jeroboam, his extreme courage was coupled with the character trait of being "industrious"—being hard-working, conscientious, energetic. Truly this is the combination that every employer or leader is wise to seek out, cultivate, and reward! Those who are willing to take on the hard task, with all their effort and in a conscientious manner, are those who can be trusted to manage both people and resources to the leader's advantage!

Give Your child, O Lord, a desire to do the most she can do, as conscientiously and energetically as she is able, and to display courage in the face of all obstacles. Let her become a person of great "valor" in a world desperate for people of valor.

270

Treats

Your comforts delight my soul.
(Psalm 94:19b NKJV)

God has an abundance of Heavenly rewards and earthly blessings for His people as a whole. We each have the privilege of partaking in ALL those rewards and blessings according to our faith and obedience. In addition, however, the Lord has unique blessings for each believer. These blessings address our soul—our mind and emotions. They are in keeping with our unique gifts, propensities, and God-given purpose. They speak to our deep desires and dreams. They give us delight, and help us experience God's love in tangible ways that assure us of His *personal* love for us. God invites all people to His feasts. Once there, He has special "party favors" for each of us!

I ask You today, Lord, to give Your beloved child a special reward or blessing—something that will be a "delightful treat." You know exactly what to give, reveal, or affirm in Your child. I trust You to be the Amazing Giver!

271

Fortitude

Man the fort!
Watch the road!
Strengthen your flanks!
Fortify your power mightily.
(Nahum 2:1 NKJV)

Fortitude is what makes us a one-person FORT in defense of the Gospel, and gives us a position of strength in our spiritual warfare against the devil. The substance of fortitude is a blend of COURAGE and FAITH. Our exterior position of fortitude is only as strong as our trust in the Lord and our willingness to express that trust in visible or tangible ways. We first must receive strength from God, and then display that strength in some way. The net result will be that we become a bulwark of strength for others.

I pray, O Lord, that You will bestow an extra measure of strength on Your servant today—strength in body, strength in mind and emotions, and above all, spiritual strength. Give him *fortitude*—the ability to walk through any and every painful or difficult situation. Make him keenly aware that His strength is an extension of Your strength. Help him to rely fully on You to carry him through!

272

The Ability to Take Full Advantage of an Opportunity

David inquired of the LORD, saying, "Shall I pursue this band? Shall I overtake them?" And He said to him, "Pursue, for you will surely overtake them, and you will surely rescue all."
(1 Samuel 30:8 NAS)

Opportunities come our way *daily*. They require our choice-making and decision-making. We must ask the Lord, "What do You want me to do, have, and be?" We are wise to ask the Lord questions that can be answered "Yes" or "No." Those are the easiest commands for us to hear—we have been hearing them from the time we were born, from parents and other adults, as well as our siblings! Listen closely. God will answer. And when He does, we can move forward with courage and conviction that He has built-in purpose and rewards for our day. We also must keep in mind that the enemy of our souls sends us "distractions" that sometimes APPEAR to be opportunities. Only God sends true opportunities for our increase, blessing, and enrichment.

Show Your child, O Lord, how she is to respond to the opportunities that come her way.

> *Prayer enables a person to shift from seeing their problem bigger than God, to seeing God as bigger than their problem.*
>
> —Anonymous

273

Knowledge about How to Manage an Opportunity

As we have opportunity, let us do good to all.
(Galatians 6:10 NKJV)

The word opportunity implies that we have been presented a combination of favorable circumstances or situations that give us a CHANCE for advancement, improvement, or increase. Every opportunity requires action on our part. And, once an opportunity begins to take root and grows, we must have wisdom about how to manage the opportunity for maximum benefit—a benefit not only for ourselves and our families, but for others around us, both in the church and in the greater "world" in which we live. Opportunities come to ALL people. But, not all people seize them and develop them. Be on the alert for what God is sending your way and take *full advantage* of the chance being given you.

Help Your servant today to see the opportunities you are sending to her *right now*. Don't let her miss an opportunity. Help her to know how to seize an opportunity and then manage it as it grows.

274

Wisdom in Managing Time

There is an appointed time for everything.
And there is a time for every event under heaven.
(Ecclesiastes 3:1 NAS)

Time is given to each person—it is the only "commodity" that every person on the earth received this morning! Ask God how best to use the hours He gives you. There is a plan and purpose for each day. We must seek it, and then fulfill it.

Heavenly Father, guide Your servant today in using every hour of every day to bring You glory and to fulfill the plans and purposes You have for Your servant's life.

275

Clean Air and Water

When they came to Marah, they could not drink the waters of Marah, for they were bitter.... Then [Moses] cried out to the LORD, and the LORD showed him a tree; and he threw it into the waters, and the waters became sweet.
(Exodus 15:23,25 NAS)

Clean air and water are vital for LIFE—and the purity of air and water directly impacts health. We must take in the highest purity of water and air possible; these two "ingestibles" are at the foundation for establishing "quality of life." If you are struggling with a health issue, address the quality of the air you are breathing and the liquids you are drinking. Simple changes can have big impact. Ask God to guide you!

Give Your child wisdom today, O Lord, about what she is to drink—and not drink. Help her to do what she can to increase the purity of the air she breathes and the fluids she drinks.

Just when I need Him, He is my all,
answering when upon Him I call;
tenderly watching lest I should fall.

—William Poole

276

Nutritious and Sufficient Food to Eat

[Jesus taught His followers to pray:]
"Give us this day our daily bread."
(Matthew 6:11 NAS)

Our daily bread includes food for our bodies, as well as food for our minds and spirits. We should take in the BEST possible, in order to be the STRONGEST possible, and to have the MOST to give to others—either as acts of our physical strength and energy, the impartation of our knowledge, wisdom, and spiritual insights, or as our prayers. Most people know the phrase, "Garbage in, garbage out." That is true in all areas of life. It is equally true, "God's best in, God's best out."

Help Your child today, Heavenly Father, to make wise choices about what she will allow into her being—into her body, her mind, and her spirit.

277

A Field Ready for Harvest

Let us not grow weary while doing good, for in due season we shall reap if we do not lose heart.
(Galatians 6:9 NKJV)

God's harvests are ensured. The *quality* and *quantity* of the harvest are partially our responsibility. We must plant the best seed, plant generously, and tend the growing process diligently. But, we can be assured that God is a Harvest Producer. He takes everything that we sow and multiplies it for our benefit and the benefit of others around us. We must not grow weary when we see little fruit from our efforts. God is at work! The time is coming! When the time of harvest comes, we must be ready and diligent in "bringing in the sheaves."

Lord, impart Your strength to Your child today so that he will want to work to the best of his ability, with expectation that You can and are using all of His effort to build Your kingdom.

278

A Relaxed Time to Enjoy God's Handiwork

O LORD, our Lord,
How majestic is Your name in all the earth,
Who have displayed Your splendor above the heavens! . . .
When I consider Your heavens, the work of Your fingers,
The moon and the stars, which You have ordained;
What is man that You take thought of him?
(Psalm 8:1,3–4 NAS)

God created all things for our use, but also our pleasure! We are to delight in the beauty, intricacy, structure, purpose, and elaborate interrelationships among all things in God's creation! We do not create. We only rearrange—our creativity is simply the reordering or restructuring of elements already created, and to a great extent, ideas already expressed. That does not mean that we have any less to offer the world or history—it does mean that we are wise to acknowledge that God alone creates and to look for the lessons in His creation that teach us more about HIM.

O Lord God, Creator of All, renew a "wonder" about Your world in the heart of Your beloved one.

279

A Welcome Call or Visit from a Beloved Friend or Relative

"Blessed are you ... as soon as the voice of your greeting sounded in my ears, the babe leaped in my womb for joy."
(Luke 1:42,44 NKJV)

When the virgin Mary went to visit her close relative Elizabeth, Elizabeth greeted her with blessing and joy! Even the baby in Elizabeth's womb reflected her joy, no doubt with an extra kick or two! Nothing cheers our hearts and souls as much as a welcome visit from a beloved friend or relative. Be such a "visitor" today to someone who would welcome the sight of you.

Help Your child, O Lord, to find an opportunity today to bring blessing and joy to someone that You love and she loves.

280

The Opportunity to Exert Godly Influence

[The apostle Paul prayed for the Thessalonians:]
Therefore we also pray always for you that our God would count you worthy of this calling, and fulfill all the good pleasure of His goodness and the work of faith with power, that the name of our Lord Jesus Christ may be glorified in you, and you in Him, according to the grace of our God and the Lord Jesus Christ.
(2 Thessalonians 1:11–12 NKJV)

What an amazing thing to fulfill all the "good pleasure of His goodness" and the "work of faith with power." God has designed us to be transformed into the nature of Christ Jesus—and it is His goodness and His miracle-working power that we are to manifest to the world. Any time we do so, Christ is glorified and we are glorified in Him!

May it be so today, dear Lord, that Your child will walk in Your ways to bring glory to Your name in all she says and does!

281

Receiving Recognition that Can Be Passed on to the Lord

"Let the Lord be glorified."
(Isaiah 66:5 NKJV)

No person accomplishes *anything* by his own power or intellect. No person can make his own heart beat or his own lungs take their next breath. God authorizes the moments of our lives, and He is the One who gives the ideas, energy, insights, and motivation to accomplish the good works that He desires to be done on this earth. Any time we think we have done something great, we are wise to acknowledge that God is doing something even *greater*.

Help Your child today, to give You glory, honor, and to yield full authority to You in all things. Let her be quick to recognize that You are the source of her life and her accomplishments.

> *Every good and holy desire, though it lack the form, hath in itself the substance and force of a prayer with God, who regardeth the very moanings, groans, and sighings of the heart.*
>
> —Thomas Hooker

282

A Cup of Cold Water on a Scorching Hot Day

[Jesus said:]
"Whoever in the name of a disciple gives to one of these little ones even a cup of cold water to drink, truly I say to you, he shall not lose his reward."
(Matthew 10:42 NAS)

Few things are more refreshing and satisfying than a glass of ice-cold water on a very hot day. This is the "refreshment" that the Lord promises to His people spiritually. It is refreshment that renews, or "makes new." Ask the Lord to give you the totality of His refreshment so that your energy and enthusiasm for His work will continue.

Father, give to Your beloved servant today a new outpouring of spiritual refreshment. Give her enthusiasm, energy, and a renewed sense of purpose for the day ahead.

283

Willingness to Go Where God Leads

Show me Your ways, O Lord;
Teach me Your paths.
Lead me in Your truth and teach me,
For You are the God of my salvation;
On You I wait all the day.
(Psalm 25:4–5 NKJV)

God has a special path for each person—it is like a "lane" on the greater path prescribed for all believers. Our goal is twofold: First, we must find the unique path God desires for us to walk individually. Second, we must trust God daily to lead us on that path so that we avoid all pitfalls, ambushes (by people or the devil), and detours. How do we discover the path that is *our* purpose and fulfillment? We ask God for it, and then wait upon God to reveal opportunities to us. When those opportunities come our way, and we know with certainty they are from God, we must get up and walk out the life He has prepared for us. God gives the map, but we must do the traveling!

Give Your servant a deep desire to do only what You ask him to do, nothing else. Give him clarity of vision when it comes to what You desire for him to undertake, and what You desire for him to lay aside. Give him patience to wait for Your insights, and to take the stance, "I won't go if I don't know."

> The value of persistent prayer is
> not that He will hear us . . . but
> that we will finally hear Him.
>
> —William McGill

284

Worship with Reverence

Serve the LORD with fear;
And rejoice with trembling.
(Psalm 2:11 NKJV)

Fear in this verse relates to deep awe and respect. We must never lose sight of God's supremacy over all things and all people. He is our Superior in every aspect of creation! Even as we rejoice at God's triumphs in us, and through us, we are to put our joy into the context of knowing that the accomplishment is God's, not ours. We should stand in amazement at the truth that He does use human beings to fulfill His purposes. He does converse with human beings. He does have regard for human beings. What an awesome truth! We must never devolve into frivolous thinking about God, nor adopt a "relating casually" demeanor toward Him.

Help Your beloved one to have even deeper respect and reverence for You today. Keep her from frivolity or casualness when it comes to Your majesty and authority.

285

A Period of High Productivity

"But now take courage ..." declares the Lord, ... and work; for I am with you."
(Haggai 2:4 NAS)

God is ultimately the One who enables all of our productivity. It is His imparted wisdom that helps us become more efficient and effective. He makes it clear throughout His Word that He is *with* us in all things, including our practical work designed to meet practical needs on this earth. We are wise to ask God to increase our productivity so that we make the most of every hour of every day, and, as the Book of Common Prayer states, "do all such good works as He has prepared for us to walk in."

Enlarge the capacity of Your beloved servant, O Lord, to do more with less effort and in less time. Increase the contribution that she can make to others around her and to the growth of Your kingdom, I pray.

Prayer often changes what
arguments cannot.

—Unknown

286

Boldness in Speaking the Name of Jesus

Every day, in the temple and from house to house, they kept right on teaching and preaching Jesus as the Christ.
(Acts 5:42 NAS)

Even after they were soundly reprimanded and warned never to speak the name of Jesus again, the apostles "kept right on." When we truly have a relationship with Christ Jesus, we cannot help but tell what we know about Him (teaching), and what we believe He has done for us and has called us to do (which means expressing in our own words and from our own experience, this truth: Christ Jesus died for us on the cross and calls us to believe in Him and receive everlasting life and forgiveness of sin). The Gospel message is not complicated. It can be learned and told by a young child! What is lacking is not experience with the Lord or the privilege of witnessing, but rather, a willingness to lay aside all fears of rejection and to speak the name of Jesus. The most effective way? Our greatest effectiveness is likely to be our speaking to those closest to us in the church pew and Sunday school classroom, and in relationships that are rooted in home fellowship groups. That's where a true Jewish learning model can take root—asking questions, hearing answers, presenting principles, and applying examples!

I ask You to give Your beloved child boldness in speaking the name of Jesus at every opportunity—of telling all she knows about You and what You have done for her and desire to do for every person. Let her days be filled with teaching and preaching opportunities, even as she undertakes the other responsibilities and work You have called her to do.

Prayer is the chief agency and activity whereby men align themselves with God's purpose.

— G. Ashton Oldham

287

Children to Love

[Jesus said:]
"Permit the children to come to Me; do not hinder them; for the kingdom of God belongs to such as these. Truly I say to you, whoever does not receive the kingdom of God like a child will not enter it at all." And He took them in His arms and began blessing them, laying His hands on them.
(Mark 10:14–16 NAS)

Every person needs a child to love—if not as a son or daughter, perhaps as a foster child or adopted child, a grandchild or godchild, a niece or nephew, or simply a neighbor child who needs an adult mentor or Sunday school teacher. A child links an adult to the next generation and to the higher purposes for passing on faith and the faith-culture of the Church. The child needs the adult for a true role model of righteous living, insights into God's Word, and the rudiments of living by faith. Having a relationship with a child—rooted in love and availability—is a win-win for both the adult and child! A person is never too old to love a "youngster."

Thank You, Father, for gifting Your servant with a baby to love and children to bless by his presence and his wisdom. Give him numerous opportunities for prayer, play, and giving the gift of "presence" to listen, share, and teach about You.

288

Grandchildren and Other "Greats"

May you see your children's children.
(Psalm 128:6 NKJV)

From ancient times, the two greatest blessings a person could experience have been children and land. Children provide ongoing legacy for a godly parent. What a privilege to nurture children in the Lord, and to teach them God's Word. This is true even for those who are childless in the natural, but who help "raise" up spiritual children to love and serve God.

Let Your beloved enjoy the children You have given to her to love. Help her to impart a legacy of loving God and loving others.

289

Appreciating without Coveting

Let your conduct be without covetousness.
(Hebrews 13:5 NKJV)

It is not a sin to *admire* something that another person has, or an honor another person wins. It is not a sin to *desire* to own or win a similar item or award. The sin of coveting manifests itself as a deep desire to have what the other person has or has earned—to the point of your having it and their NOT having it. Coveting tends to be an all consuming obsession, which readily destroys relationships and fuels greed and envy. The key? Admire, but then work hard to earn what you desire.

Father, please free Your child from all covetous impulses. Help her to admire without coveting.

> No prayer of adoration will ever soar
> higher than a simple cry: "I love You, God."
>
> —Louis Cassels

290

Building Up Your Spiritual Self

Building yourselves up on your most holy faith, praying in the Holy Spirit, keep yourselves in the love of God, looking for the mercy of our Lord Jesus Christ unto eternal life.
(Jude 20:21 NKJV)

Every Christian faces the challenging of building up himself or herself spiritually. We do that by exercising our faith—trusting God to do what we cannot do, and believing for God to do great things—by praying in the Spirit, by keeping God's commandments, and by looking always for Christ's mercy—bestowed on us, and also on others. These are not automatic "givens" or automatic desires in the Christian's heart. They must become goals that are pursued and desires that are cultivated. God will do His work in us, but only if we are willing to do the spiritual-formation work that He sets before us.

Give Your child a heart today, O Lord, to build up his spiritual being—to exercise faith, pray deeply, obey fully, and accept mercy.

291

God's Definitive Defeat of an Enemy

[Moses said to the people:]
"Do not fear! Stand by and see the salvation of the LORD . . . for the Egyptians whom you have seen today you will never see them again forever."
(Exodus 14:13 NAS)

We may do battle with our enemies—in the spiritual realm and at times in the natural realm—but we must always be aware that it is

God who authorizes and accomplishes ALL victories. He is the One who saves us *definitively* from those who seek to undermine, limit, or persecute us. We are wise to ask God to eliminate our enemies from our lives, and at the same time, to trust Him to do with our enemies what *He* desires. He will either remove them from us or transform them so they are no longer enemies!

Enlarge the trust of Your beloved child when it comes to Your miracle-working, enemy-defeating power, O Lord. Give her confidence to stand firmly, and in awe, that You are winning the battle on her behalf.

292

Specific Guidance for a Right Decision

Your righteousness shall go before you;
The glory of the LORD shall be your rear guard.
(Isaiah 58:8 NKJV)

We are to be led by righteousness—by a sense of what is RIGHT before God, and a sense of what will KEEP us in right relationship with God. When we do this, the Lord's presence will guard us from enemy attack, and also provide safety for those who may be following our lead. It is vital that we have God's clear direction in our choice-making and decision-making. Only His approved path will yield maximum success and safety.

Give Your beloved one guidance for today. Help him in all his decisions. Protect him in all ways from enemy attack.

Prayer unites the soul to God.

—Julian of Norwich

293

Godly Prosperity

Beloved, I pray that you may prosper in all things and be in health, just as your soul prospers.
(3 John 2 NKJV)

God's plan for prosperity covers the *whole* person. It is not limited to material or financial provision. It is to begin with spiritual prosperity. It includes health, which is both physical and emotional "well-being." To prosper means to flourish or thrive. It is to live life to the fullest—as Jesus said, to live an "abundant" life. (See John 10:10.) Prosperity is vitality, overflowing physical and mental energy that includes a joyful spirit and optimism for all opportunities. It is not at all selfish or greedy to pray for God's prosperity. Indeed, prosperity is the highest quality of LIFE, and God desires that we seek His best!

Grant Your prosperity to Your child today. Let her be exuberantly joyful in the life You impart to her!

294

Godly Success

Happy is the man who finds wisdom,
And the man who gains understanding;
For her proceeds are better than the profits of silver,
And her gain than fine gold.
She is more precious than rubies,
And all the things you may desire cannot compare with her.
(Proverbs 3:13–15 NKJV)

Wisdom is the key to knowing HOW to act in all situations, including how to invest, how to manage finances and people, how to conduct business affairs, and how to spend and save one's earnings for maximum benefit. Many people "luck" into money, through a variety of means, but the earning of money takes understanding about money and God's wisdom for how to regard money. With wisdom, success in EVERY area of life is guaranteed—and it is whole-person success that is GODLY success. Money cannot produce any of the good things a person desires to have for one's entire life and into eternity—it does not automatically secure health, family happiness, or loving relationships, including a reconciled relationship with God. Wisdom, on the other hand, can lead a person to pursue and experience all that truly matters in LIFE and ETERNITY.

Grant, O Lord, wisdom to Your beloved servant so she will truly grasp YOUR concept of success and be eager to pursue it.

295

Health and Protection for a Beloved Pet

Blessed shall be . . . the increase of your herds, the increase of your cattle and the offspring of your flocks.
(Deuteronomy 28:4 NKJV)

Personal blessing in the Old Testament was always extended to a blessing on what the person owned, including their animals. Many of the animals that we consider to be sources of "food" were not actually eaten frequently in Old Testament times. Sheep, for example, were herded for their *wool* far more than for their meat; goats were herded for their hair and their milk, more than for meat. Both sheep and goat lambs were often given names at their birth and were treated as pets.

Help Your child today to be a good steward of any animal You have entrusted to her care, for whatever purpose. Please be the protector and healer of those animals that are Your creation! Help Your beloved one to be a good "care-giver."

296

Choosing Life and Prosperity over Death and Adversity

[Moses spoke these words from the Lord:]
"See, I have set before you today life and good, death and evil, in that I command you today to love the LORD your God, to walk in His ways, and to keep His commandments, His statutes, and His judgments, that you may live and multiply; and the LORD your God will bless you in the land which you go to possess."
(Deuteronomy 30:15–16 NKJV)

Whenever we are in a life or death situation, we must battle valiantly for LIFE. This requires an activation of our will. We are to CHOOSE life. We are to base this choice on our understanding of God's infinite love and mercy, His absolute commands, and His promise to bless us and be with us. God desires that we live a high-quality life every hour of our ordained years so that we do all He has authorized for us to do in multiplying His message of love and forgiveness to the world. Our focus must be on God's help for LIFE and His promises of an ABUNDANT LIFE. We must not rehearse what is negative, adverse, or troublesome, but focus our thoughts, words, and deeds on what is positive, productive, and holds the potential for blessing.

Give Your beloved child a renewed awareness that every day is filled with life-or-death decisions, most of them small. Every choice moves us toward blessing and increase, or toward cursing and decrease. Help Your child to choose LIFE, O Lord.

297

Good Health

Your light shall break forth like the morning;
Your healing shall break forth speedily.
(Isaiah 58:8 NKJV)

God desires that we each wake up renewed, refreshed, and full of energy every morning! He desires that we have sufficient strength to do all that He has prepared for us to do in any given day. Our part is to make right choices regarding what we eat, drink, and the ways in which we sleep and handle stress. God's part is to impart *life* to us, and to protect us from all forms of disease that might try to invade our bodies, minds, and spirits. Trust God to do His part as we do our part.

Give your beloved child the health that is necessary to do the work You desire to do in the world today—both *in* your beloved child, and *through* your beloved child. Give him energy, strength, and enduring power.

298

Quickness in Learning

"Learn to do good."
(Isaiah 1:17 NAS)

God desires that we learn what is GOOD. The more clearly we have defined and are in pursuit of good, the easier it is to spot an evil counterfeit or a lie. Where do we find God's definitions about what is good? In God's Word! Moses said, "Hear, O Israel, the statutes and the ordinances which I am speaking today in your hearing, that you may learn them and observe them carefully." (Deuteronomy 5:1 NAS) We learn with our minds, and what we learn mentally becomes a "way of thinking" that frames our decisions and choices. The end lesson, however, lies in the *application* of what we learn. We learn the most when we apply what we believe to the thorny and difficult circumstances and needs of daily life. We can trust God to help us in both *knowing* what to do, and actually *doing* what is good.

O Lord, help Your child today to learn what is good and to be quick to do it! Help her to be a "quick study" when it comes to knowing right from wrong, and to be courageous in doing only what is right.

299

Staying on Task

[The apostle Paul wrote:]
I press on so that I may lay hold of that for which also I was laid hold of by Christ Jesus . . . forgetting what lies behind and reaching forward to what lies ahead. I press on toward the goal for the prize of the upward call of God in Christ Jesus.
(Philippians 3:12–14 NAS)

It is one thing to know what God desires for a person to be and to do. It is another thing for that person to actively *pursue* what God desires. And, it is yet another thing to *continue* to pursue—to persevere and to endure in pursuit—those things that God desires. God is in the process of making us into the people with whom He wants to live forever, but He requires that we participate in the process! Faithfully, consistently, and ardently.

Help Your child, O Lord, to stay on track with what You have commanded and what You desire. Infuse him with new energy and new desire to become all You want him to be in this world. Help him to accomplish all the good works that you have set before him as Your goals.

300

Feelings of Fulfillment

Take heed to the ministry which you have received in the Lord, that you may fulfill it.
(Colossians 4:17 NKJV)

True fulfillment comes through service to others as the Lord leads and empowers us. His purpose for us, above any career or personal purposes, is that we might use all of the talents and abilities He has given to us as a benefit and blessing to others. As we give ourselves away, we find that *we* are "fully filled" with joy, satisfaction, and meaning for life.

Lead Your beloved one to the ministry You desire for her, and then empower her to do that ministry with excellence. Impart to her deep feelings of fulfillment and satisfaction for a life of service.

301

Open Doors

[Jesus said:]
Knock and it will be opened to you . . . to him who knocks it will be opened.
(Matthew 7:7b-8 NKJV)

We are the ones who must "seek entrance" into the deeper truths of God's Word and the nearer presence of the Lord. When we actively seek God, He immediately opens Himself to us. It was a tradition of Jesus' time for those who hosted a traveling rabbi to open their homes after the evening meal so that all in the community might avail themselves of the opportunity to meet and learn from the rabbi. A simple knock at the gate meant a sure welcome to enter the evening's discussion about God's Word.

Give Your child the desire to knock on the door of Your heart, Lord—with full confidence that You will welcome her into a deeper understanding of Your plans and purposes, Your love, and Your abiding presence.

302

A Willingness to Take Up Christ's Yoke

[Jesus said:]
"He who does not take his cross and follow after Me is not worthy of Me."
(Matthew 10:38 NKJV)

The crosspiece that a convicted person "carried" toward a Roman crucifixion site was tantamount to a "yoke"—it was a piece of wood draped over the shoulders of the criminal or person being executed for their rebellion against Rome. Jesus called upon His followers to be willing to die for the sake of the Gospel. Part of that commitment was to live each day as if "under the yoke" of service and witness in the name of the Lord.

Help Your child today, O Lord, to take on Your identity and to carry You into the world—pouring out her life in service and witness, willing to die if necessary for Your sake.

303

Assuming a Position of Leadership when Necessary

For this reason I left you in Crete, that you should set in order the things that are lacking, and appoint elders in every city as I commanded you.
(Titus 1:5 NKJV)

The apostle Paul appointed Titus to a leadership position, one that involved "setting things in order" and appointing a chain of authority (elders). The role of the top leader in a church is still to make sure that what is taught and preached is theologically correct, and to make sure good leaders are in charge of all service programs. Leadership always requires an ability to organize and to choose the right people for key positions. If you are called to assume a leadership position, you can trust God to equip you for the task—revealing to you what you need to know in order to be effective. Don't complain if a person in authority over you, as Paul was over Titus, asks you to assume a leadership role. Rather, trust God to help you fulfill that role in a way that pleases Him fully.

O Lord, give Your child a deep awareness that You will help her be the leader that others have appointed her to be. Give her insights into how to organize and work with people. Give her peace about the role You have established for her.

304

Being a Good "Follower"

Remember those who rule over you, who have spoken the word of God to you, whose faith follow, considering the outcome of their conduct.
(Hebrews 13:7 NKJV)

The Bible calls us to follow godly men and women—both those who have preceded us in history, as well as those in authority positions today. The Bible never calls us, however, to follow *blindly*. We are to follow the word of God spoken to us—as long as the Word (the Bible) has been spoken to us fully and correctly. And, we are to follow the behavioral examples of others—as long as the "outcomes of their conduct" prove to be truly righteous. We are wise to look over the shoulders of those who are leading us to see the road ahead, and to align what we see with the call of God on all Christians and on us individually and specifically. Ultimately, the Lord calls us to follow Christ Jesus with our whole heart, mind, soul, and strength, and to follow the daily directives of the Holy Spirit. We MUST be good followers before we can ever be genuine disciples (students and representatives).

Help Your beloved one today, O heavenly Father, to be a good follower—diligent in doing all that You direct and diligent in helping others whom You have appointed.

305

Trusting God for Lasting Success

Now to Him who is able to keep you from stumbling,
And to present you faultless
Before the presence of His glory with exceeding joy,
To God our Savior, Who alone is wise,
Be glory and majesty,
Dominion and power,
Both now and forever.
Amen.
(Jude 24-25 NKJV)

This passage, often called the Jude Benediction, is a tremendous tribute to Christ Jesus, and also a checklist for those attributes that we must trust the Lord to impart to us! He alone is able to keep us from stumbling in our faith journey or falling into temptations; He alone is our source of joy, wisdom, and spiritual power. He alone is worthy of all praise and worship. He alone brings us to eternal life. He alone causes His glory to be reflected in us. This is a picture of "lasting success"—a legacy of success that transcends our lifetime. May we pursue it with our whole heart!

Father, give Your child a deep desire to pursue those things that YOU authorize for both time and eternity. Help her to turn to You continually to lead, help, and secure her lasting legacy of godliness.

306

Finding the Answer

[Jesus said:]
"Seek, and you will find . . . he who seeks finds."
(Matthew 7:7-8 NKJV)

Of all the things that human beings seek, three of the most prevalent are these: inner peace, eternal purpose, and loving relationships. Jesus is the ultimate in each of these categories! He alone give us the "ultimate" peace—but only as we diligently seek to be reconciled fully to the Father and to pursue those things that make a person whole. Jesus alone gives us eternal purpose—life in heaven, and on earth, life abundant—but only as we turn to Him for direction as given by His Holy Spirit. Jesus alone gives us a lasting loving relationship—but only as we are willing to receive His love. The work of Christ Jesus in us is not an automatic "given," but it can be ours if we will seek, and keep on seeking Him. God does not play "hide 'n' seek" with us. He delights in being "found" by us, but He does not force Himself on us.

Reveal Yourself today, O Lord, to Your faithful and seeking child.

307

The Planting of Good Seed in Good Soil

[Jesus spoke in a parable:]
"Other seed fell on good ground and yielded a crop that sprang up, increased and produced: some thirtyfold, some sixty and some a hundred."
(Mark 4:8 NKJV)

God produces harvests from seed. Our role is to plant good seed in good soil, and then to cultivate the seeds that emerge as plants. God's role is cause a seed to grow and to produce a harvest from it. Each seed directly produces fruit or grain that is greater, or has the potential to be greater, than the seed itself. God gives us the seed necessary for the harvest He desires to produce. Every good farmer knows it is imperative to take a portion of a harvest and set it aside as the seed for a future harvest. The best of the harvest makes the best seed! We are wise to ask the Lord to reveal to us the best part of our harvests for the purposes of replanting. This teaching of Jesus applies, of course, to the spiritual realm as much as to the natural realm.

Give Your child a joyful anticipation when it comes to seed-planting and reaping harvests from You. Show her how to manage the harvests You give to ensure future good harvests. Help her to trust You fully throughout all the planting and cultivating processes related to projects, business opportunities, and ministry activities.

More things are wrought by
prayer than the world dreams of.

—Alfred, Lord Tennyson

308

Good Leaven

[Jesus said:]
"The kingdom of heaven is like leaven, which a woman took and hid in three measures of meal till it was all leavened."
(Matthew 13:33 NKJV)

The challenge of Jesus was for each person to spread the Good News of His life throughout the person's broader society or culture—to proclaim what He taught and what He did *widely*, in both word and deed. And then, we as individuals are to trust the Holy Spirit to use our words and deeds as a "leavening" agent—expanding the whole of the loaf of the culture or society for good.

Help Your child today, O Lord, to spread the good leaven of Your truth!

309

Rest for the Soul

[Jesus said:]
"Take my yoke upon you and learn from Me, for I am gentle and lowly in heart, and you will find rest for your souls. For My yoke is easy and My burden is light."
(Matthew 11:29-30 NKJV)

Every yoke in ancient times was carved *especially* for the animal that was going to wear it. Thus, the yoke fit perfectly, and did not chafe or cause wounds to the animal as it did its work. It was "easy" to carry. God has a unique purpose for each person, and He has gifted each person in unique ways to fulfill that purpose. Thus, when we are in the "groove" of doing what we have been created to do, for causes that are eternal, we do not see our work as a burden, but as a joyful pursuit! Our minds and emotions are energized by what we do and by seeing how God uses our work and service to bless others.

Show Your beloved servant today a way to do the work You have created her to do in a way that is productive, beneficial, and joyful!

310

An Accurate Roadmap or Blueprint

Now may our God and Father Himself, and our Lord Jesus Christ, direct our way to you.
(1 Thessalonians 3:11 NKJV)

God not only gives us a vision that is related to a goal He desires for us to pursue. He also gives us the *way*—the means, the "how to"—we are to follow as we pursue His vision. His plan gives us the details we need so that we not only arrive at His designated destination, but build or establish things that are to His specification, and along the way, influence others for the Gospel. God does not want us to fail or fall short of His excellence. God's Word, the Bible, is our ultimate roadmap or blueprint for how to live.

Give Your beloved child today, O Lord, a sense that you are leading him step by step, and that You will provide all the details necessary for him to do Your bidding for the greatest possible excellence and effectiveness.

Prayer is not overcoming God's reluctance;
it is laying hold of His highest willingness.

—Richard C. Trench

311

The Healing of a Broken Heart

[Jesus said:]
He has sent Me to heal the brokenhearted.
(Luke 4:18 NKJV)

Jesus saw one of His fulfillments of Isaiah's prophecy about the Messiah (Isaiah 61:1-2) as that of healing those who were brokenhearted. To be brokenhearted is to be in mourning over the loss of something considered of high value—perhaps grief at the death of a loved one, the loss of a relationship, or the loss of a valued career or possession. God's desire is that we know and receive *His presence* as the balm for our loss, disappointment, and the feelings associated with the "void." He will fill us with Himself if we will ask Him to do so. His presence *heals*—it restores, it renews, it rebuilds.

Heal any area in Your child today that is in mourning over a loss. Restore, renew, and rebuild her from the inside out so that she truly can *know* Your presence and radiate Your joy.

312

Recovery from Dashed Hopes and Dreams

I wait for the LORD, my soul does wait,
And in His word do I hope.
My soul waits for the Lord
More than the watchmen for the morning,
Indeed, more than the watchmen for the morning.
(Psalm 130:5–6 NAS)

The challenge to "wait" in this passage refers to a patient expectation that God is about to do something new and wonderful in a person's life. God's promise is one day closer to being manifested or fulfilled! We are to watch for the new beginning, new burst of energy and health, new harvest, or new reward just as a young child eagerly awaits the dawn of Christmas morning!

Increase the expectation level of Your child today, I pray. Give her an enthusiasm and confidence that what You have said You will do is truly what You ARE DOING!

313

Enduring to the End

[Jesus said:]
"He who endures to the end shall be saved."
(Matthew 24:13 NKJV)

The word "saved" in this verse does not refer to a person's eternal spiritual reconciliation with God the Father. It refers to a "deliverance that makes perfect." The words for saved and healed come from the same root in the Hebrew. They are words that bring a person to wholeness. Those who endure life's struggles, with full confidence and trust in God, are those who experience God's delivering and perfecting power. They are the ones who are made whole.

Help Your child today, O Lord, to endure all of the pain, hardship, and persecution that come her way so she might be perfected and delivered by You—and emerge from times of trouble and trial even stronger in faith and more effective in her witness.

314

Building on a Solid Foundation

You are no longer strangers and foreigners, but fellow citizens with the saints and members of the household of God, having been built on the foundation of the apostles and prophets, Jesus Christ Himself being the chief cornerstone, in whom the whole building, being fitted together, grows into a holy temple in the Lord, in whom you also are being built together for a dwelling place of God in the Spirit. (Ephesians 2:19–22 NKJV)

Every person who believes in Jesus Christ as Savior is part of something bigger than himself or herself! That person is part of Christ's entire body—the church around the world, including all Christian denominations that have members of all races, language groups, and cultures. Jesus is the only One who can fit the entire "peoples puzzle" together. He is the only One who knows the unique contribution of each person, and of each group of believers. What good news—we have a worldwide family, and we are no longer "strangers or foreigners" to one another! We each have the same "older brother" in Christ Jesus. This gives us solidarity, and strength.

Give Your beloved one a sense of Your abiding, undergirding strength, and show her how this strength comes from You through others who believe in You and are serving You. Help her to be a strength in return to others in her family of Christ.

315

Companionship

I am a companion of all who fear You,
And of those who keep Your precepts.
(Psalm 119:63 NKJV)

Choose your "companions" carefully! The word companion literally means with (com) bread (pan). Companions in Bible times were those with whom a person broke bread, which in the ancient world was a sign of great hospitality. Hosts who welcomed a person into their home for a meal took on a responsibility to protect and provide for that guest as long as the person remained in their home. It was vitally important for a person to judge the character of a person before inviting him in for a meal—the safety of the home and family members depended on good judgment. The same is true for today.

Give Your beloved one sweet companionship with the right kinds of friends. Let a mutuality of protection and provision flow in her friendships.

316

Alertness

[Jesus said:]
"Be watchful, and strengthen the things which remain, that are ready to die."
(Revelation 3:2 NKJV)

We are to be ready at all times for the Lord to call us home to Himself, or to return to make His home with us on this earth! Either way, we are homeward bound. We are called by God to be watchful in all things, and to be especially alert to those things that should remain beyond our lifetime. When it comes to establishing or reinforcing lasting values and traditions, we must be keenly aware of those things that are on the verge of dying or are in the process of dying—and we must take action that they do not die! We must continue to nurture and to strengthen the values, beliefs, and traditions that uphold Christ Jesus and extend the Gospel to those who do not know Him. We must continue to nurture and strengthen the newfound faith of young believers and the children who are growing up in our churches. We must not let the flame of faith go out!

Help Your beloved child today, O Lord, to be watchful over all things and to be a genuine caregiver and nurturer of those things that You want to establish on this earth. Help her to produce an exceedingly great and good fruit that will last FOREVER.

317

Carefulness in Exalting God, not Possessions

"Beware that you do not forget the LORD your God by not keeping His commandments . . . otherwise, when you have eaten and are satisfied, and have built good houses and lived in them, and when your herds and your flocks multiply, and your silver and gold multiply, and all that you have multiplies, then your heart will become proud and you will forget the LORD your God."
(Deuteronomy 8:11–14 NAS)

Genuine and lasting success comes with a pricetag: *full obedience* to all of God's commandments and to His daily directives spoken into our hearts by the Holy Spirit. No person who willfully chooses to disobey God can expect God's blessings, no matter how excellent their efforts or "open" their mind might be. Take care in the way you deal with what has been entrusted to you (not only as material goods and financial resources, but as talents and spiritual gifts). Ask God for His wisdom in how to maximize all that you have for your good and the good of others around you. We must always exalt God, *not* ourselves, what we accomplish, or what we possess.

O Lord, help Your child to be "careful" with the resources You have given to her and to remember always that obedience to You is the first requirement for good management.

318

Speedy Recovery

The prayer of faith will save the sick, and the Lord will raise him up.
(James 5:15 NKJV)

The words "heal" and "save" are interchangeable in many passages of the Bible—they come from the same root word in Hebrew. Faith-filled prayer has healing power, something the Western modern mind is just beginning to verify by its scientific and medical methodologies. The Lord is the One who raises people up from sickness and sin. He responds to faith, not need or circumstance.

Help your child today, O Lord, to be an agent of Your healing power—praying for others with faith. Help Your child to turn quickly to those who will pray with faith any time a need arises in her life.

319

Being a Willing Worker

[Jesus said:]
"Whoever desires to be first among you, let him be your slave—just as the Son of Man did not come to be served, but to serve, and to give His life a ransom for many."
(Matthew 20:27–28 NKJV)

God may not ask us to pour out our blood as martyrs for the Gospel, but He does ask us to pour out our life's energy and abilities for the Gospel! We must give our ALL to serve others in Christ's name. It is the least we can do for the Savior who poured out His life as a ransom for us, that we might enjoy full forgiveness and reconciliation with our Heavenly Father, and live with God in Heaven one day. We are to be WILLING slaves to God's service.

Give Your beloved one a heart to serve—to work hard and long, and to give his very best, for the sake of the Gospel.

320

Seeing Obstacles as Opportunities

[Jesus said:]
"To him who overcomes I will grant to sit with Me on My throne, as I also overcame and sat down with My Father on His throne." (Revelation 3:21 NKJV)

We see obstacles in our path as either impediments or challenges; we will be stopped by them or look for ways to tunnel under them, soar over them, go around them, or bore through them! It is only when we see the obstacles in our path as a gauntlet cast by the enemy of our souls that we will use spiritual means to turn obstacles into opportunities. Don't let the devil stop you. Overcome him by the power of your faith, by giving testimony to your witness about Christ, or by quoting the Word of God.

Give Your beloved servant the ability to see what YOU desire to accomplish in every obstacle that appears in her path. Give her overcoming faith, a strong witness, and a skillful knowledge and remembrance of Your Word.

Nothing lies beyond the reach of prayer except that which lies beyond the will of God.

—Unknown

321

A Heart Made Glad

My heart also instructs me in the night seasons.
I have sent the LORD always before me;
Because He is at my right hand I shall not
be moved. Therefore my heart is glad.
(Psalm 16:7–9 NKJV)

The foremost time for study and discussion of God's Law was during the three-hour period immediately after sundown—in other words, after dinner and before bedtime. What was taken in of God's Word became the context and prelude for sleep, and was thought to be the substance spawning godly dreams and visions that often occurred during sleep. When we "set the Lord before us" as the sole object of our devotion and service, He gives us lasting confidence and joy— He guides us waking, and guards us sleeping.

Heavenly Father, give Your child sweet sleep, filled with the truth of Your word. Assure her always that Your strong right hand is protecting her whether she is awake or asleep. Give her joy, in her daily walk, and in her nightly slumber.

322

Peace within the Family

Behold, how good and how pleasant it is for brethren to dwell together in unity.
Psalm 133:1 KJV

This verse certainly refers to a person's immediate family—and we all know that when families are in agreement about values, behaviors, schedules, and "family agendas," all members of the family benefit. The psalmist, however, lived in a world of tribal communities—at least twelve "varieties" of what it meant to be an Israelite. The peace that can come from unity within a family was regarded as essential for peace in the nation that King David ruled. We can liken this need for unity and peace to various Christian denominations today. We must find accord on the essentials of our faith, refusing to let differences related to style and protocol divide us. Only then will we find our ecumenical efforts "good" in God's eyes and "pleasant" in the realm of our own experience.

Help Your beloved child today to be an agent of peace within the Church—promoting the essentials of the faith and not the differences that divide. Let her experience the goodness of Your plan for the Church and the joy of being in deep relationship with others.

323

Innocence

[Jesus said:]
"Be shrewd a serpents, and innocent as doves."
(Matthew 10:16 NAS)

Why would God call upon His people to be like a "serpent?" This has nothing to do with evil, or the devil's imagery as a serpent. Snakes generally seek to avoid danger. They are quick to slither away when they sense that either a human being or a known predator is coming close. It is in that manner that we are to be "shrewd." We need to know how to avoid evil. Doves, on the other had, were considered the most innocent of all birds—never attacking, living in fidelity with their mates, and singing sweetly. Innocence is never considered to be "denial" or "lack of awareness," but rather, a sweetness of demeanor that seeks peace, not conflict.

Give Your child today, O Lord, an ability to be acutely aware of evil, but never a party to it or a cause of it.

324

Ardent Pursuit of Potential

I press toward the goal for the prize of the upward call of God, in Christ Jesus.
(Philippians 3:14 NKJV)

Each person has been given talents and gifts from God the Father, both natural gifts and spiritual gifts to be used within the church. The potential related to ALL of our gifts lies in our relationship with Christ Jesus. The deeper our relationship with Him, the more we will have the wisdom, energy, strength, and ability to use our gifts. The more we use our gifts, the more our potential is exercised and developed. A person can never fulfill his or her potential completely. There is always a need to "press" toward the goal.

Today, O Lord, give Your servant a deep desire to keep *pressing* toward all that You desire for him to be and to do. Help him to use his God-given gifts to their max.

> Prayer changes everything: It changes the one who prays, and it changes the one prayed for.
>
> —William G. Johnsson

325

Freedom from Fornication, Adultery, and Illicit Sensuality

[Jesus said:]
"From within, out of the heart of men, proceed evil thoughts, adulteries, fornications, murders, thefts, covetousness, wickedness, deceit, lewdness, an evil eye, blasphemy, pride, foolishness. All these evil things come within and defile a man."
(Mark 7:21–23 NKJV)

All of the "sins" in this passage begin with a *thought* that is in some way harbored as a fantasy, desire, or feelings of vengeance. These are sins that are subject to man's will, and therefore, are man's responsibility to address and confess. We must never be confused on the point of our sin nature—it is *never* God's desire that we sin. He sent Jesus to redeem us from sin. We must never think about sin, "God made me this way." No—the generations past made a person with certain propensities toward evil. Jesus came to change us so that we are NOT in bondage to those thoughts and desires that lead to sin. It is our responsibility to ask God to forgive us and cleanse us, and then, by the power of the Holy Spirit resident within us, to help us lead a new life that is not marked by either sinful desire or sinful deed.

Impart understanding and strength to Your servant today, O Lord, to help her turn from sin and pursue what she knows is right in Your eyes. Give her a quickness to confess sin and be forgiven of it. Purify her and help her to amend her habits of thought and desire so that she truly might change her habits of behavior.

> *When we depend on man, we get what man can do; when we depend on prayer, we get what God can do.*
>
> —Anonymous

326

Freedom from Slander, False Witness, and Undo Criticism

Whoever hides hatred has lying lips,
And whoever spreads slander is a fool.
(Proverbs 10:18 NKJV)

Slander, the bearing of a false witness (legal testimony), and undo criticism all stem from the same source—deep inner hatred and anger, often a seething form of bitterness. The person who is filled with hate never sees the full scope of God's love, and therefore cannot fathom the full scope of God's forgiveness and truth. Words spoken from a well of bitterness are always half-truths. We are called as God's people to speak WHOLE truth, which is truth that produces wholeness in ourselves and others. The person who defames others doesn't seem to realize that such words always come back around in double force. To criticize others is to invite criticism. To testify falsely against others is to invite judgment. To slander is to invite lies told about one's self.

Free Your child today, O Lord, from hatred and anger that produces bitterness. Cleanse her deep within and help her to live free of all forms of negative speaking.

327

A Quickness in Admitting Faults, Flaws, or Failures

[Jesus said:]
"Agree with your adversary quickly, while you are on the way with him, lest your adversary deliver you to the judge."
(Matthew 5:25 NKJV)

The cost of making peace is nearly always less than the cost of going to war. Even if you are "right" in your actions or decisions, you may never be able to prove fully that you are right. God knows. Most of the population doesn't care. Your adversary likely will never agree with your assessment of the situation. Be quick to admit your faults, flaws, or failures. Take ownership of at least "part" of any problem. And find a way to move forward—in peace.

Help Your beloved one today, O Lord, to find a peaceful resolution for any conflict he faces. Give him a willingness to seek peace and be an agent of peace. Give him a willingness to admit failures, flaws, and faults and to work with a mediator if necessary to bring an out-of-court settlement.

328

A Quickness in Asking for Forgiveness

[Jesus said:]
"If you forgive men their trespasses, your heavenly Father will also forgive you. But if you do not forgive men their trespasses, neither will your Father forgive your trespasses."
(Matthew 6:14–15 NKJV)

Trespasses are the sins we willfully commit against others—we cross the boundary of their life and trample on their turf in some way, just like those who fail to heed "No Trespassing" signs and unlawfully invade another's property. God requires us to forgive those who trespass against us if we have any hope that He will forgive our trespasses. We *must* forgive others. It is a command.

Help Your child today, O Lord, to *want* to forgive, and to seek to make amends with all whom she has wronged. Help her to release those who have hurt her or caused her loss. Give her a quickness in asking for, and receiving, forgiveness.

329

Refusing to Wallow in Negative Emotions

Let all bitterness, wrath, anger, clamor, and evil speaking be put away from you, with all malice. And be kind to one another, tenderhearted, forgiving one another, even as God in Christ forgave you.
(Ephesians 4:31–32 NKJV)

Negative emotions lie at the root of many illnesses. Foremost among these negative emotions are hatred, wrath, bitterness, resentment, and prejudice. All of these are emotions that sink deep into the soul and tend to seethe and ferment over time. They erupt eventually, and the damage they cause can be severe. When you feel you are wronged, go immediately to God and ask for His help. "Let go" of the offense. Choose to respond to the offender with genuine kindness. The person who has wronged you may not change, but you'll be better off!

Show your servant, O Lord, that it is entirely possible for someone to disagree with him without his thinking they have become an enemy. Remove all feelings of vengeance, hurt, and bitterness from his heart. Give him peace.

330

Maintaining Eternity-Based Priorities

"Hold fast what you have till I come. And he who overcomes, and keeps My works until the end, to him I will give power over the nations."
(Revelation 2:25–26 NKJV)

Different perspectives yield different appraisals of any situation. A close-up lens will show one view; a telephoto lens another. Jesus gave the admonition above to John for the church in Thyratira—an admonition to all believers today that we must choose God's priorities over our own perspectives. It is God's will and His works that must be kept—not our own will and works. We must "hold fast" to the faith that has been delivered to us, and to continue to cherish with high value the work of the Holy Spirit in our lives. Keeping the commands of God, and relying on His daily work in our lives, is what prepares us to rule and reign with Jesus one day.

Help Your child, Heavenly Father, to keep her eyes on You and to weigh all earthly decisions in the light of eternity. Help her to see the big picture, the long view, the telephoto picture of Your plans and purposes. Help her to see how he fits in, and what You desire for him today.

331

Displaying Respect and Being Respected

[The LORD said:]
I will have respect unto you, and make you fruitful, and multiply you, and establish my covenant with you.
(Leviticus 26:9 KJV)

Respect in the Bible is a word that means to "show favor." We show favor for a person based upon their *position* of authority over us, and especially if they occupy that position with godly judgments and compassionate care. The Lord desires to favor us and make us fruitful, multiplying our example to others around the world. His covenant through the shed blood of Jesus is for that very purpose—that His people might lead the way in establishing righteousness on the earth.

Give favor to Your child today, Lord, and cause her to be respected among her peers for her goodness and godliness. Multiply her efforts in winning the lost and edifying the saints.

332

Actively Clothing the Naked and Feeding the Hungry

[Jesus said:]
"Come, you blessed of My Father, inherit the kingdom prepared for you from the foundation of the world: for I was hungry and you gave Me food; I was thirsty and you gave Me drink; I was a stranger and you took Me in; I was naked and you clothed Me; I was sick and you visited Me; I was in prison and you came to Me."
(Matthew 25:34–36 NKJV)

The kingdom of God has no "need" because, in the kingdom of God, believers are meeting the needs of one another as God provides His provision, protection, and wise counsel! We cannot blame God for world hunger, polluted waters, loneliness, lack of adequate clothing or shelter, sickness (physical, mental, or emotion), or for false imprisonment (legally, emotionally, or spiritually). These are all "conditions" that God has given us the power and challenge to remedy!

Heavenly Father, empower Your child today to be an agent of healing, reconciliation, and need-meeting on this earth. Give her insights and wisdom into *how* to work within Your kingdom to bless others and to deliver them from all manner of bondage and need. Enlarge her capacity and ability to show Your love in ways that are healing and conciliatory.

Prayer moves the hand that moves the world.

—John Aikman Wallace

333

Peace with Others in the Church

Let the peace of God rule in your hearts, to which also you were called in one body; and be thankful.
(Colossians 3:15 NKJV)

The Body of Christ is to function as a family *without* family feuds! This is only possible when each member of the family does three things: allows the peace of God to rule their own heart, acknowledges that all believers are in one spiritual family, and gives thanks always for God's mercy and grace extended to each member of the family. Peace is *manifested* as every member of God's family uses their God-given gifts and talents to fill the roles that God has designated for them, and to serve others in those roles with generosity and perseverance.

Give Your child a desire for Your peace to rule his heart and the hearts of all those in his extended family—the blessed company of all faithful believers in Christ Jesus!

334

Eagerly Looking for Christ's Next Appearance

Let us not sleep as others do, but let us be alert and sober.
(1 Thessalonians 5:6 NAS)

As believers today we must continue to be on the alert for Christ's "second coming," but also for Christ's "next coming." Surely He appears countless times in the course of any given day—by the power of His Holy Spirit, present to do His healing, delivering, saving, and restoring work! We should live in a constant state of joyful anticipation at Christ's *next* appearing, even in this very hour.

Lord, help Your beloved servant to be on high alert in anticipation of Your next appearing in his life.

335

Joyful Anticipation of Christ's Second Coming

He who testifies to these things says, "Yes, I am coming quickly." Amen. Come, Lord Jesus.
(Revelation 22:20 NAS)

The cry of the first-century church was "Maranatha!" This was an Aramaic or Syriac expression that meant "our Lord cometh!" It was a word of tremendous hope that Jesus would soon appear again. With certainty we can know this: we are one day closer to the Second Coming of Christ than we were yesterday.

Help Your beloved child, O Lord, to be ready for Your next appearing and to live in joyful anticipation of Your revealed presence and power—today and always.

336

Tears Giving Way to Joy

Weeping may endure for a night,
But joy comes in the morning.
(Psalm 30:5 NKJV)

God's people are never commanded to refrain from weeping or from sorrow. They *are* commanded to trust God in the midst of all situations and circumstances, and to believe that the joy of the Lord can and will be experienced in the *aftermath* of sorrow and tears. We must not tell others who are sad to "snap out of it," but rather, to believe that God still has good things ahead for them, and that He loves them always. Encourage others to believe for a return of joy to their hearts.

Use the tears of Your child, O Lord, to cleanse her of sorrow and to renew within her a hope for joy to return and conquer sadness.

337

Contending for the Faith

Contend earnestly for the faith which was once for all delivered to the saints.
(Jude 3 NKJV)

To contend is to "struggle on behalf of." It is to argue for the truth, to debate or dispute. A *presentation* OF the truth of our faith turn into a *contention* FOR the faith when lies or heresy appear. In his letter to the first-century church, Jude states that ungodly people have crept into the church. They are denying Jesus Christ as Master and Lord and have turned the grace of God into licentiousness (allowing for the pursuit of sexual desires unchecked by morality or God's commandments). Jude admonishes the believers to contend *earnestly*—vigorously, as if in a battle that has life or death consequences. Indeed, any time heresy takes root, the consequences are ones of ETERNAL life and death.

Help Your beloved servant today, O Lord, to contend for the faith any time he is confronted with lies about Who Jesus is or what God commands. Give him courage to undertake the challenge, and wisdom for the debate.

338

Overcoming Procrastination, Sloth, and Laziness

He who is slothful in his work is a brother to him who is a great destroyer.
(Proverbs 8:9 NKJV)

Some things are subject to destruction because of direct attack, warfare, or some form of verbal, spiritual, or emotional assault. Other things are destroyed because they simply are allowed to decay or go unrepaired through lack of interest, diligence, or active caring. Either way—assault or apathy—destruction is destruction. We must not allow laziness, sloth, or procrastination to keep us from actively building up ourselves or others in faith, and then acting on that faith to do what God asks of us.

Give renewed energy and conviction to Your child today, Heavenly Father, that she might continue to be inspired and eager to face the faith challenges of each day. Help her not to procrastinate or to become lazy when it comes to doing what You have commanded. Help her to follow through on all the directives of the Holy Spirit with diligence and enduring strength.

339

Remembering God's Many Benefits and Goodness

Bless the LORD, O my soul, and forget not all His benefits.
(Psalm 103:2 NKJV)

What are the benefits that the psalmist wants us to remember? He lists these in Psalm 103: God forgiving or your iniquities (your inherited propensities to sin); God healing you of diseases (physical, mental, emotional, and spiritual); God redeeming your life from destruction; God crowning you with lovingkindness and tender mercies (giving you people who will love you and help you); God satisfying your mouth with good things (not only food and beverage, but words that speak life to others); and God renewing your youth. What an amazing list of "benefits" that are offered to the person who will believe in Christ Jesus and eagerly *receive* all that God desires to give! Only God can provide these benefits without failure.

Help Your beloved one to trust You for all of Your benefits, and to pursue eagerly all the things that You delight most to give.

340

Confidence in God's Trustworthiness

Jesus Christ is the same yesterday and today and forever.
(Hebrews 13:8)

The TRUTH of Jesus is an abiding, absolute truth. It does not change. This "truth" is not only the truth of what Jesus taught and commanded, but also the truth of His very life—the composite meaning of Who He Is as a person of the Trinity, and His role as the substitutionary sacrifice for the sin of mankind. What Jesus was at the foundation of all creation—the Word of God—has not and will not change. Jesus is not subject to editing. He is God. Because of this, we can have total confidence that everything Jesus purchased for us on the Cross, and all that He has promised to do in us, through us, and for us, including His gift of the Holy Spirit to us, is CURRENT. We can live in Christ today, just as Christians have lived and moved and had their being in Him for two thousand years.

Father, give Your child a renewed awareness that Jesus is as relevant to her life today as He has been to the lives of millions of people throughout history. Jesus is in the NOW of her day. Help her to trust Jesus for all that He promises in the Bible.

341

A Loyal Confidant

He who goes about as a talebearer reveals secrets,
But he who is trustworthy conceals a matter.
(Proverbs 11:13 NAS)

Few things hurt as much as a person you trusted revealing your secrets. We all have a need to confide in others; it is an integral part of marriage and friendship. We must be cautious, however, that we choose our confidants with care—never trust a person who has a reputation for gossip or who freely tells all he or she knows. The problem with tale bearing is that a talebearer thinks he is speaking "truth," which is never possible. Only God knows the full truth of any matter; human beings deal in partial truth, always subject to human interpretation and MISinterpretation. Even verifiable facts do not add up to truth, because they do not reveal meaning, intent, or the full context of the person's life.

Help Your child today, Heavenly Father, to keep secret what she is told in confidence.

> Much prayer, much power. Little prayer, little power.
>
> —Peter Deyneka

343

Active Care of Widows, Orphans, and Strangers

The alien, the orphan and the widow who are in your town, shall come and eat and be satisfied, in order that the LORD your God may bless you in all the work of your hand which you do.
(Deuteronomy 14:29 NAS)

The Law of Moses had strong admonitions for the Israelites to extend kindness to all widows, orphans, and strangers. The people were held responsible for those in their community who had no family member to care for them, provide for them, or protect them. We in the church are to make our own widows, parentless children, and the strangers who have sought refuge in our midst our TOP PRIORITY when it comes to charitable giving and deeds of provision (food, clothing, shelter, and fellowship).

Help Your child, O Lord, to be generous in seeking out and helping to meet the needs of those in the church who need assistance. Help her to be alert to needs even before a needy person asks for help.

344

Good Neighbors

Let each of us please his neighbor for his good, leading to edification
(Romans 15:2 NKJV)

We do well when we show kindness to our neighbors, helping them in practical ways that are for their *good*. Such acts of kindness are honored by God and bring reward back to those who give. In the end, both the neighbor who gives and the neighbor who receives are "built up" (edified) in their spirit, and are better able to bear the fruit of kindness in dealing with those who live beyond the neighborhood! In the early church, a neighbor was one who "lived close," often a guest in the home, a fellow slave or co-worker, or a fellow church member. It is to our neighbor that we give our "first witness" beyond our family members. They are the front line of our lives when it comes to evangelism and ministry. We should aim to give what our neighbors are willing to receive, not limiting our giving to any one dimension of life, but at the same time, not pressing our gifts into hands (or hearts) that don't want to receive them.

Give Your child wisdom today, O Lord, about how to be a good neighbor. Show her what to give and how to give it. Build up her faith and witness in the community where she lives, I pray.

345

Active Visitation of Prisoners and Those in Hospitals

[Jesus said:]
"I was sick and you visited Me; I was in prison and you came to Me... inasmuch as you did it to one of the least of these My brethren, you did it to Me."
(Matthew 25:36, 40 NKJV)

This verse certainly includes hospital and prison visitation—telling the Gospel, having an active prayer ministry, engaging in Bible study, and encouraging those who are ill and incarcerated. The verse goes beyond those ministries, however. Any person is in "prison" if he or she is confined emotionally or physically. Any person is "sick" if any area of his life is subject to disease, discouragement, or diminishment. The sick and imprisoned are also those who are homebound, including those who are too filled with shame to go out in public, who are unable to function in the greater community owing to a mental or emotional illness, or who are incapacitated by an injury or sickness. We are to go to them with the good news of

God's love, and to minister to them in the name of Jesus. Our first priority is to do this for the brethren, those who are our fellow believers in Christ Jesus.

Help Your child today, O Lord, as he goes to minister to those who are sick and imprisoned. Give him wisdom, joy, and compassion. Help him to be a source of encouragement, healing, and restoration.

346

Seeing All Circumstances as Being Under God's Control

"We give You thanks, O Lord God Almighty,
The One who is and who was and who is to come,
Because You have taken Your great power and reigned."
(Revelation 11:17 NKJV)

God is on His throne 24/7. Our Creator remains in control of all aspects of His creation at all times. He is never taken by surprise or forced to do anything that is opposed to His plans and purposes. In the believer's life, God does not merely "allow" certain things to happen. He causes things to happen and His goal is always to bring eternal reward and earthly benefit to His child. In truth, we cannot make things happen in our strength. We do not fully control anything. We will be either a participant with, or obstruction to, God's desires. In any circumstance, relationship, or situation, therefore, we must yield our will to God's will and say, "Lord, use me in whatever way You can to bring glory to Your name, to win lost souls to Your kingdom, and to build up Your saints."

Give Your child assurance today, O Lord, that You are the creator of all things—including the circumstances of today—and that You are in control *always*.

347

Believing for God to Work ALL Things to Good

We know that God causes all things to work together for good to those who love God, to those who are called according to His purpose.
(Romans 8:28 NAS)

Nothing is ever wasted from God's perspective. He uses all that we think, believe, experience, say, and do to transform us into the people with whom He wants to live forever, and to further His plans and purposes on this earth (through us and around us). God's plans are *always* for our good—our eternal reward and our earthly blessing. If you question whether you are among those who are "called" according to His purpose, the answer is a resounding "yes." Trust God to do His work in every area of your life.

Help Your child today, O Lord, to trust You in every circumstance and relationship. Help her to embrace Your eternal work, aware that it is for her good. Help her to wait for You to reveal to her Your plans before she rushes ahead to fulfill her own dreams. Use her, Lord, as she remains faithful and obedient to You.

The first purpose of prayer is to know God.

—Charles L. Allen

348

An Unsullied Reputation

Be blameless and harmless, the sons of God, without rebuke, in the midst of a crooked and perverse nation, among whom ye shine as lights in the world.
(Philippians 2:15 KJV)

No person can avoid making errors and mistakes; we are each flawed and frail. We live in a fallen world. But, we can seek to live in a way that is blameless and harmless *in God's eyes*. Others may blame us; others may try to tag us with their own sins or project their faults on us, but the only opinion that counts in the long run is God's opinion! He will use our purity, transparency, and truthfulness, as a light *of His* wattage and voltage to shine His love and mercy into the hearts of people who are estranged from Him.

Heavenly Father, help Your beloved servant to live blameless and harmless in Your eyes. Use his life as a beacon drawing others away from evil and toward You.

349

Accepting the Lord's Pruning

[Jesus said:]
"Every branch in Me that does not bear fruit He [the Father] takes away; and every branch that bears fruit He prunes, that it may bear more fruit."
(John 15:2 NKJV)

The keeper of the vine is God the Father! His goal is to produce divine fruit in us, in order that His fruit might nourish others and be replicated. In order to have the most productive vineyard, a farmer must cut away all dead wood that keeps sun from getting to the live wood, and prune branches to produce a greater flow of sap thus, increase fruit production. In the spiritual realm, it the Holy Spirit who enables our witness to shine more clearly, and who seeks to remove all obstacles within us that keep us from hearing and heeding His directives fully. Pruning may be painful at times, but it is always God's intent to make us more productive in the ways He desires us to help fulfill *His* plans and purposes.

Help Your beloved one to yield today to Your pruning, Heavenly Father. Do Your work in her and through her. Help her to give You the glory always!

350

Stillness in Spirit

Be still, and know that I am God.
(Psalm 46:10 KJV)

The busy brain, and the busy body, are self-focused. Activity requires self-focus in order to do things in an orderly, efficient, and logical manner. Self-focus, however, limits a person's awareness of God and therefore, a person's ability to be *totally* God-focused. This perhaps is one of the reasons that people close their eyes when they pray—they are shutting out the stimuli that activate brain and body, so they might concentrate more completely on the Lord. To be "still" means to shut OUT external stimuli and even the thoughts related to "things to do" and "problems to solve." It means capturing every thought and emotion and subjecting it to a *God-focus*. Being "still" is a requirement for truly *knowing* the fullness of the I AM. It is also one of the most difficult things for most believers to do!

Help Your beloved child today, O Lord, to be still in order to know You more fully and more intimately.

Prayer—secret, fervent, believing prayer—
lies at the root of all personal godliness.

—William Cary

351

Abundant Treasure Stored Up in Heaven

[Jesus said:]
"Provide yourself money bags which do not grow old, treasure in the heavens that does not fail, where no thief approaches nor moth destroys."
(Luke 12:33 NKJV)

So many things that we consider to be "treasures" now simply won't matter at all to us once we are in eternity. Sadly, the pursuit of those earthly treasures can often keep us from devoting full-time energy and talent toward investing in the things that DO count forever. And even sadder still, the acquisition of the things we consider to be earthly treasures often results in disappointment. The Bible tells us clearly that there are only two things that last forever—God's Word and those who believe in Christ Jesus. Our pursuit of a greater understanding of God's truth, and our pursuit of an ever-deepening relationship with the Lord are what truly COUNT!

Help Your child, O Father, to put her time, energy, and talent into those things that truly last—into relationships that are eternal and into learning and applying Your eternal truth. Give her what she needs for this life, but help her not to regard those things as being life-giving. Only You are the Lord, the Giver of Life!

352

Full Provision of All that Is Necessary

[The Lord said through the prophet Isaiah:]
"For as the rain and snow come down from heaven,
And do not return there without watering the earth
And making it bear and sprout,

And furnishing seed to the sower and bread to the eater;
So will My word be which goes forth from My mouth."
(Isaiah 55:10–11a NAS)

There isn't anything you need that doesn't already exist in abundance in Christ Jesus. He who made the worlds as the Word of God knows how to direct all provision and protective resources to you. He knows the beginning and ending of all circumstances. He knows all solutions and answers. He fully empathizes as the incarnate Christ who suffered and died. Rather than pray for more provision, pray for Jesus to act on your behalf!

Jesus, provide all that Your child needs today.

353

Quickness in Valuing Others

Honor all people. Love the brotherhood. Fear God. Honor the king.
(1 Peter 2:17 NKJV)

Christ-followers must deal regularly with strangers, fellow believers, the Lord, and those in authority over us. The Bible gives very focused and specific ways of addressing these four groups of people: show RESPECT (honor) to everybody, friend or stranger. GIVE and show affection to those who are fellow Christians. This does not mean we give exclusively to fellow believers, but rather, that the Body of Christ is to be our priority in areas of practical ministry. To "FEAR" God means to express the utmost awe and reverence for God—we worship Him and Him alone. And finally, we are to HONOR (respect) those in authority over us—even if we disagree, we are to disagree in peace. Even as we work to change laws and bring about greater justice, we are to obey the existing laws and judicial regulations as long as they do not bring us into direct opposition to God's law. Those who follow these ways of valuing others around them have the best possible opportunity to live a peaceful, productive life.

Help Your child today, O Lord, to treat others as You command. Help Your child to show respect to all, and to above all, worship only You.

354

Taking Responsibility for One's Own Actions

I acknowledged my sin to You,
And my iniquity I have not hidden.
I said, "I will confess my transgressions to the LORD,"
And You forgave the iniquity of my sin.
(Psalm 32:5 NKJV)

When we accept responsibility for our own sins and failures—not trying to blame others, justify our actions or thoughts, or dismiss as unimportant the offenses we cause—God is quick to forgive us. (In the New Testament, 1 John 1:9 mirrors this truth.) There is an interesting use of terms in this verse. The psalmist acknowledges that what he has done has separated him from God—it is *sin*. He then states that he has faced up to his own propensity to sin, the inborn desire for sin that he inherited from his forefathers. This he terms *iniquity*. He states that he has *transgressed* against other people and that he has confessed this to God. In turn, God has forgiven—wiped clean, removed—the psalmist's propensity to sin in that particular way. We are responsible for seeking forgiveness of others when it comes to our transgressions, but once we have done this, God quickly forgives us *and* transforms us so that we feel far greater conviction any time we are about to "transgress" in that way in the future.

Forgive Your child today, O Lord—quickly and freely, as You have promised—for those transgressions and sins confessed to you.

Cleanse Your child of the propensities to sin that have been inherited from generations past. Renew a right spirit in Your child!

355

Truly Desiring the Best for Others

Mercy, peace, and love be multiplied to you.
(Jude 2 NKJV)

In every relationship, we do well to pray this prayer from Jude. Every person needs more, and ever more, of God's mercy, His peace—which is the shalom of wholeness and perfect reconciliation with Him, and His loving kindness expressed by His favor, blessings, and near presence. In the end, nothing matters as much as knowing God is merciful in dealing with us, and that he loves us and is in the process of making us whole.

Let Your servant today experience even more of Your mercy, peace, and love, O Lord!

356

Laying Claim to All God's Promises and Blessings

She [wisdom] is a tree of life to those who take hold of her,
And happy are all who retain her.
(Proverbs 3:18 NKJV)

The verse immediately preceding this one gives three great benefits of wisdom, which is called the fruit of the "tree of life." First, length of days; second, riches and honor; and third, a pleasant life marked by pervasive "pleasant days" and peace (wholeness). Having "length of days" means that a person finds fulfillment and joy in old age—just living a long life is not a blessing if a person does not have the health, loving relationships, and faithful friendship with God to make those days a true blessing. The wise person is at peace with God, enjoys what God gives, and is a person who delights in the pleasures of life that come about through greater and greater wholeness.

Help Your child today, O Lord, to lay claim to all that You have promised and desire to give. Help her to pursue wisdom and to enjoy its wonderful fruit!

357

Having a Ready Answer for the Questions You Are Asked

Always be ready to give a defense to everyone who asks you a reason for the hope that is in you, with meekness and fear.
(1 Peter 3:15 NKJV)

Bible study—from cover to cover, in full context—not only prepares us for eternity, but also helps us to know HOW to answer those who ask us about Christ Jesus. When others want to know why we have hope in the midst of a world that seems to be spinning out of control toward the side of evil, we need to have an answer. As we give our answers, with humble awe of God and in agreement with the Holy Spirit's leading, our words can make the difference between heaven and hell for other people. Some questions don't require an answer other than a quote from the Bible. Other questions require personal testimony. Every believer is pre-qualified to give both!

When questions come, impart Your answers to Your child, O Lord. Let her be quick to give testimony to you and to use Your word as her finest defense or explanation.

358

A Growing Friendship with God the Father

The LORD spoke to Moses face to face, as a man speaks to his friend. (Exodus 33:11 NKJV)

Very few people are described as friends of God in the Old Testament. (See James 2:23.) Jesus, however, said to His disciples on the night before His crucifixion, "You are My friends" (John 15:14). Jesus invited His disciples to enter *His* relationship with the Father. What do friends do? They spend time together. They share intimate secrets with one another regarding their goals, dreams, and desires. Friends help one another to fulfill their plans and purposes. They acknowledge one another and are loyal to one another. In all these ways, we truly can be "friends" with God the Father.

Today, O Lord, impart to Your child a deeper understanding of what it means to be Your friend.

359

Having a Greater Desire to Imitate Jesus the Son

Beloved, now we are children of God; and it has not yet been revealed what we shall be, but we know that when He is revealed, we shall be like Him, for we shall see Him as He is. And everyone who has this hope in Him purifies himself, must as He is pure.
(1 John 3:2–3 NKJV)

We aren't like Jesus yet, but we each should be in pursuit of *becoming* more and more like Him in character every day! To that end, we are to keep ourselves pure, confessing all that is revealed to us as sin. The more we "see" Jesus for Who He is, the more we are to model ourselves like Him, seeking to become such a good copy of Christ Jesus that others see us as "in the image of Christ" (which is what the word "Christian" means). We each imitate those whom we perceive to be in authority over us, or perceive to be worthy of our intense admiration and respect. Our number-one authority and role model is Christ Jesus!

Give Your child a desire today, Heavenly Father, to be more like Jesus. Convict him of his need to purify his life and to come into full alignment with Christ. Help him to see Jesus clearly with unclouded spiritual eyesight.

360

Having a Greater Reliance upon God the Holy Spirit

Do not quench the Spirit.
(1 Thessalonians 5:19 NKJV)

To "quench" the Spirit is to dismiss, disregard, or disavow the Spirit's presence, or to treat the Spirit's directives with indifference or only half-hearted attempts at obedience. In modern-day terms, to quench is to "throw cold water onto a hot fire." The opposite of "quenching" is to place increasingly high regard and reliance upon the Holy Spirit for comfort, counsel, and ongoing conviction about evil! We are either growing cooler in our relationship with God the Holy Spirit, or warmer. May we each develop a red-hot glow, with no desire to stop the flow of God's work in us and through us!

Kindle Your Spirit anew in the life of Your beloved one, I pray, O Lord. Give her a deep desire to burn with Your love for all things that You value, including lost souls You desire to birth into Your kingdom!

Humility is the principal aid to prayer.

—Teresa of Avila

361

Tenacity in Holding onto What God Says Is Good

Test all things; hold fast what is good.
(1 Thessalonians 5:21 NKJV)

Discerning good from evil is often a challenge, especially in a world where good is often called evil and evil is called good. Our culture seems to be increasingly deceived. The challenge of knowing what God calls "good," however, can be met! The key is to know the Word of God thoroughly, and to read and study it from cover to cover. Once we know what GOD says is good, we must build our lives on those principles and declare those truths boldly.

Help Your beloved servant today, O Lord, to study Your word and to apply it to daily life, testing all things in the culture against the veracity of Your truth. Help Your servant to CLING to what is good and to refuse to compromise Your truth.

362

Prudence and Discretion

See that no one renders evil for evil to anyone, but always pursue what is good both for yourselves and for all.
(1 Thessalonians 5:15 NKJV)

Prudence and discretion are words that relate directly to how we are to treat others in practical ways. "Prudence" means to have good sense in managing material resources and making sound decisions regarding relationships—the word is often equated with avoiding unnecessary risk. To have "discretion" means to deal with situations sensitively in order to avoid embarrassing others or needlessly upsetting others. It includes the ability to keep another person's secrets. Both prudence and discretion require that refused to be self-absorbed—rather, we seek to do what is beneficial for all who are in association with us in our family, church, and neighborhood. The prudent, discreet person is always a welcome asset to any community!

Help Your child today, O Lord, to be prudent and discreet.

363

Fully Yielding the Kingdom, Power, and Glory to God

[Jesus taught His disciples to pray:]
Yours is the kingdom and the power and the glory forever. Amen.
(Matthew 6:13 NAS)

The version of the Lord's Prayer found in Matthew (see also Luke 11:2–4) ends with a "yielding" to God the Father of all that pertains to His Kingdom, His power, and His glory. The Kingdom is simultaneously on earth and in heaven—only God rules over it. Its citizens are totally under His authority at all times. God alone has absolute power, including power of understanding and wisdom, power of creative expression, and all power over time (especially its beginning and ending in a person's life). God alone is worthy of all glory—all praise, all respect, all honor, all worship. In other words, we might pray, "God, Yours is EVERYTHING!" God creates all, governs all, possesses all, and is worthy of honor for all. We live to serve Him, now and forever. He is Source and King. Does this make us unimportant? Far from it. We are in close intimate relationship with the Ruler of the Universe! What a wonderful position to be in!

Receive the praise of Your servant, O Lord. Reveal anew the many ways in which You govern Your kingdom, use Your awesome power, and are worthy to receive ALL praise, thanks, and expressions of exaltation. Help Your servant to rejoice and delight that You are the Almighty King who is also her loving FATHER.

364

An Identity Wrapped Up in the Life of Christ

In Him we live and move and exist.
(Acts 17:28 NAS)

We have no claim to *any* aspect of our personhood. Our personalities, our natural talents and spiritual gifts, our opportunities, our abilities and capacities, our very breath and heartbeat come to us from God the Creator, spoken into our lives by the breath of God and framed into a unique language only for our ears by Christ the Word! It is within the IDENTITY of Christ Jesus that we live, both now and in eternity. All that we do, say, and think must be brought into alignment with His will and His love.

Help Your child today, O Father, to embed herself so completely in Christ Jesus that she thinks as Jesus thought, speaks as Jesus spoke, loves as Jesus loved, and does only what the Holy Spirit directs her to do.

365

Loving God with All One's Heart, Soul, Mind, and Strength

[Jesus said:]
"'You shall love the Lord your God with all your heart, with all your soul, and with all your mind.' This is the first and great commandment."
(Matthew 22:37–38 NKJV)

Jesus frequently quoted the Book of Deuteronomy, and this statement is one that is found in Deuteronomy 6:5—"You shall love the LORD your God with all your heart, with all your soul, and with all your strength." The passage in Deuteronomy goes on to tell us specific ways to express love to God: keep all of His commandments, statutes, and testimonies; remember and teach His commandments to future generations; revere only God and worship only Him; refuse to follow other gods or make idols to them; refuse to test Him, and choose to do all that is right and good in the sight of the Lord. When we keep the commandment to love God, we are in a position to keep all other commandments, and to follow the daily directives of the Holy Spirit. To "love God" is to praise Him, thank Him, and acknowledge Him as the Source of our life, and at all times, give Him the honor due His name!

Help Your child today to keep You FIRST in her life, in all ways and at all times. Help her to love You FIRST, to acknowledge You with thanks FIRST, to give praise to You FIRST, and to make Your directives her FIRST priority for any given day.

366

Glimpses of the Will of Heaven Becoming Reality on Earth

[Jesus taught His disciples to pray:]
"Thy kingdom come, Thy will be done in earth, as it is in heaven."
(Matthew 6:10 KJV)

Our template for life on earth is to live according to the way we will live forever! Heaven functions according to God's commandments, with every person in Heaven *obeying fully* and *loving generously*. These two concepts are at the very heart of worship. The more we learn about how Heaven functions, the greater our desire is likely to grow for starting to practice the "Heaven Lifestyle" today.

Give Your child a deeper insight into Heaven's lifestyle, and then, a deeper conviction to change things in his own life to conform to Heaven's way!

> *Genuine prayer is never "good works," an exercise or pious attitude, but it is always the prayer of a child to a Father.*
>
> —Dietrich Bonhoeffer

> *O Lord . . . fill up all that is wanting, reform whatever is amiss in me, perfect the thing that concerns me. Let the witness of your pardoning love ever abide in my heart.*
>
> —John Wesley

ABOUT THE AUTHOR

Jan Dargatz, Ph.D., has been writing about Bible themes for more than thirty-five years, and has taught adult Sunday school classes on a regular basis for most of that time.

She says, "I PRAY for those I teach—and specifically, I pray for the Holy Spirit to do in their lives the work HE desires to do. I have no doubt whatsoever that this is a prayer the Lord delights in answering. God's desires are always in complete alignment with Holy Scripture. And therefore, prayers that pray for the Truth of God's Word to come alive in and be applied by a person, are prayers God will ALWAYS answer in a positive way. I have absolute confidence about that! God's answers are always creative, always exciting, and always unique to the person. What an adventure to participate in God's plans and purposes through prayer!"

Other books by Jan Dargatz

These books by Jan—with more insights into prayer—are currently or soon to be on Amazon.com in Kindle or print versions.

Thou Shalts—More than 400 Positive Bible Commands with Insights

Gates of Thanks and Courts of Praise—A Journey in Prayer

Discover the Secrets of Sweet Sleep

Peering over the Rim of the Rut—Aspiring to More

Praise A-Z—Creative Pathways for Daily Praise

Making the Choice for Joy!—You can experience deep inner joy—regardless of what's happening around you.

www.ingramcontent.com/pod-product-compliance
Lightning Source LLC
LaVergne TN
LVHW051824080426
835512LV00018B/2720